A Russian in the Woods

Peter Whelan was born in the Potteries in 1931. His plays include *Captain Swing* (RSC The Other Place, Stratford, 1978), *The Accrington Pals* (RSC Pit, London, 1981), *Clay* (RSC Pit, London, 1983), *The Bright and Bold Design* (RSC Pit, London, 1991), *The School of Night* (RSC The Other Place, Stratford, 1992), *Shakespeare Country* (Little Theatre Guild, 1993), *Divine Right* (Birmingham Rep, 1996), *The Herbal Bed* (RSC The Other Place, Stratford, 1996, West End and New York), *Overture* (New Vic, Newcastle-under-Lyme, 1997) and *Nativity* (Birmingham Rep, 1999). Television includes *The Trial of Lord Lucan* and *In Suspicious Circumstances*. He is married, has two sons and a daughter, and lives in London.

Methuen Drama

3 5 7 9 10 8 6 4 2

First published in 2001 by
Methuen Publishing Limited

A CIP catalogue record for this book is availabe from the British Library

ISBN 0 413 76610 1

Typeset by SX Composing DTP, Rayleigh, Essex

A Russian in the Woods

by

Peter Whelan

Methuen Drama

THE ROYAL SHAKESPEARE COMPANY

The Royal Shakespeare Company is probably one of the best-known theatre companies in the world. It has operated in its present form since 1961 when it changed its name from the Shakespeare Memorial Theatre Company, established a London base and widened its repertoire to embrace works other than Shakespeare.

Today the RSC has five home theatres. In Stratford the Royal Shakespeare Theatre stages large-scale productions of Shakespeare's plays; the Swan, a galleried Jacobean playhouse, brings to light the plays of many of his neglected contemporaries alongside classics of world theatre, while The Other Place, the company's studio theatre, houses some of the company's most exciting experimental and contemporary work, as well as providing a regular venue for visiting companies and some of the RSC's education work, including the annual Prince of Wales Shakespeare School.

In 1982 the company moved its London home to the Barbican Centre, where in the large-scale Barbican Theatre and the studio-sized Pit Theatre, the company stages new productions as well as the repertoire transferring from Stratford.

But Stratford and London are only part of the story. Recent years have seen a dramatic increase in the reach of the RSC, with major RSC productions on tour around the UK and abroad. Productions from Stratford and London visit regional theatres, while our annual regional tour continues to set up its own travelling auditorium in schools and community centres around the country. This ensures that the RSC's productions are available to the widest possible number of people geographically. An extensive programme of education work accompanies all this, creating the audiences of tomorrow by bringing the excitement and the power of theatre to young people all over the country. Between November 2000 and June 2001 the RSC will have presented over 40 weeks of theatre in more than 25 towns and cities in the UK, outside our own theatres.

In the past few years the company has taken Shakespeare to enthusiastic audiences in Europe, the USA, Australia and New Zealand, South America, Japan, India and Pakistan, Hong Kong, Turkey and Korea. The RSC is grateful to The British Council for its support of its overseas touring programme.

Despite enormous changes over the years, the company today continues to function very much as an ensemble of actors and actresses, whose artistic talents combine with those of the world's top directors and designers and the most highly-skilled technical teams to give a distinctive and unmistakable approach to theatre.

THE OTHER PLACE

The Other Place is the RSC's smallest theatre. The theatre also houses our rehearsal studios and has a central role in the history of the RSC as a centre for research and development.

Our roots lie in two distinct areas. In the early 1960s Michel St Denis brought to the company the European tradition of 'the actors' laboratory' and worked with actors, directors, writers, designers and technical staff to develop singly and together their own craft and imagination and that of the company.

While the company continued to explore ways of revealing Elizabethan drama, actors and directors sought new audiences for new work. Theatregoround was born. This was the first small-scale work the company had done and it laid the foundation for subsequent seasons at The Roundhouse and The Place in London. The 'tin hut' became The Other Place and Buzz Goodbody its first artistic director. In 1991 we outgrew the tin hut and moved to our present purpose-built home.

This season we celebrate our tenth anniversary in this theatre with the production of three new plays. David Edgar and Peter Whelan continue their long association with the RSC and Martin McDonagh joins them to complete our trilogy of new writing for the new century.

Since its inception The Other Place has produced work by many of the major contemporary dramatists: Edward Bond, Howard Brenton, Nick Dear, Peter Flannery, Christopher Hampton, Mike Leigh, David Rudkin, Willy Russell, Charles Wood, and more recently, Biyi Bandele, April de Angelis, Anne Devlin, Pam Gems, Robert Holman, Bernard-Marie Koltes, Derek Walcott, and Nigel Williams. This season our current exhibition in the café reflects this unique body of new writing.

Alongside these the classical balance has been maintained with new productions of European classics and Shakespeare. As well as new plays in performance, we run workshops with young writers, giving them the chance to work with RSC actors on themes which reflect the concerns of the classical repertoire.

In the present-day TOP we remember Buzz Goodbody and Michel St Denis in the rehearsal rooms named after them and their legacy continues in our developmental work. Each year we work with actors to assemble a programme of workshops focusing on different disciplines. We are members of the Union of European Theatres and RSC actors, directors and designers regularly meet their European counterparts for an exchange of ideas.

Steven Pimlott
Director of The Other Place

THE ROYAL SHAKESPEARE COMPANY

RSC EDUCATION

The objective of the RSC Education Department is to enable as many people as possible from all walks of life to have easy access to the great works of Shakespeare, the Renaissance and the theatre.

To do this, we are building a team which supports the productions that the company presents onstage for the general public, special interest groups and for education establishments of all kinds.

We are also planning to develop our contribution as a significant learning resource in the fields of Shakespeare, the Renaissance, classical and modern theatre, theatre arts and the RSC. This resource is made available in many different ways, including workshops, teachers' programmes, summer courses, a menu of activities offered to group members of the audience, pre- and post-show events as part of the Events programme, open days, tours of the theatre, community activities, youth programmes and loans of parts of the RSC Collection for exhibitions.

We are building, for use world wide, a new web site to be launched this year. This will make available all of the above, as well as providing access to the RSC's collection of historic theatre and Shakespearean material. It will also carry interesting and interactive material about the work of the RSC.

We can also use our knowledge of theatre techniques to help in other aspects of learning: classroom teaching techniques for subjects other than drama or English, including management and personnel issues.

Not all of these programmes are available all the time, and not all of them are yet in place. However, if you are interested in pursuing any of these options, or for information on general education activities, contact Education Administrator Sarah Keevill on 01789 403462, or e-mail her on sarah.keevill@rsc.org.uk.

JOIN THE RSC

For £8 a year you can become an RSC Associate Member. Benefits include:
* Advance Information and priority booking for our Stratford and London seasons (plus the RSC Residency if you live in the appropriate area).
* Special priority booking subscription scheme for the Stratford Summer Festival Season.
* Deferred payment facilities on Stratford tickets booked during the priority period (by instalments with a credit card).
* Special Members' performances for some Stratford and London productions.
* No fees payable on ticket re-sales in Stratford.
* Free RSC Magazine

Full members
For £24 all of the Associate benefits, plus:
* Guaranteed seats for RSC productions in the Royal Shakespeare Theatre, Swan Theatre and Barbican Theatre (for tickets booked during the priority period).
* An extra week of priority booking for Stratford and London seasons.
* 10% discount on purchases from RSC Shops.

Group and **Education** membership also available.

Overseas Members
The RSC tours regularly overseas. In recent years we've visited the USA, South America, Japan, India and Pakistan, as well as most parts of Europe. Wherever you are in the world, you can become an RSC Member. Overseas Membership is available from £15.

Special Overseas Members
All the benefits of a Full Member, plus:
* A complimentary programme for each Royal Shakespeare Theatre production.

For further information write to the Membership Office, Royal Shakespeare Theatre, Stratford-upon-Avon, CV37 6BB or telephone 01789 403440.

STAY IN TOUCH
For up-to-date news on the RSC, our productions and education work, visit the RSC's official web site: **www.rsc.org.uk**. Information on RSC performances is also available on Teletext.

A PARTNERSHIP WITH THE RSC

The RSC is immensely grateful for the valuable support of its corporate sponsors and individual and charitable donors. Between them these groups provide up to £6m a year for the RSC and support a range of initiatives such as actor training, education workshops and access to our performances for all members of society.

The RSC is renowned throughout the world as one of the finest arts brands. A corporate partnership offers unique and creative opportunities both nationally and internationally, and benefits from our long and distinguished record of maintaining and developing relationships. Reaching over one million theatregoers a year, our Corporate Partnership programme progresses from Corporate Membership to Business Partnership to Season Sponsor to Title Sponsor, and offers the following benefits: extensive crediting and association; prestigious corporate hospitality; marketing and promotional initiatives; corporate citizenship; and business networking opportunities. Our commitment to education, new writing and access provides a diverse portfolio of projects which offer new and exciting ways to develop partnerships which are a non-traditional and mutually beneficial.

As an individual you may wish to support the work of the RSC through membership of the RSC Patrons. For as little as £21 per month you can join a cast drawn from our audience and the worlds of theatre, film, politics and business. Alternatively, the gift of a legacy to the RSC would enable the company to maintain and increase new artistic and educational work with children and adults through the Acting and Education Funds.

For information about corporate partnership with the RSC, please contact:
Liam Fisher-Jones
Development Director
Barbican Theatre
London EC2Y 8BQ
Tel: 020 7382 7132
E-mail: liamfj@rsc.org.uk

For information about individual relationships with the RSC, please contact:
Graeme Williamson
Development Manager
Royal Shakespeare Theatre
Waterside, Stratford-upon-Avon CV37 6BB.
Tel: 01789 412661
E-mail: graemew@rsc.org.uk

You can visit our web site at **www.rsc.org.uk/development**

A Russian in the Woods was first performed by the Royal Shakespeare Company
at The Other Place, Stratford-upon-Avon, on 21 March 2001, supported by RSC Patrons.
The cast was as follows:

Anthony Flanagan	Pat Harford
Colin Mace	Clive Burns
Stuart Goodwin	Reg Dilke
Charlie Simpson	Geoff Wirral
Anna Madeley	Ilse Bucher
Louis Hilyer	Fraser Cullen
David Hinton	Dieter Stahl
Douglas Rao	Lloyd Jackson

Directed by	**Robert Delamere**
Designed by	**Simon Higlett**
Lighting designed by	**Rick Fisher**
Music by	**Harry Peat**
Movement by	**Terry John Bates**
Dialect Coach	**Charmian Hoare**
Company voice work by	**RSC Voice Department**
Production Manager	**Mark Graham**
Costume Supervisor	**Christopher Porter**

Stage Manager	**Simon Dodson**
Deputy Stage Manager	**David Marsland**
Assistant Stage Manager	**Marisa Ferguson**

GHOSTS OF BERLIN

Long distance memories are like silent movies...sounds often get edited out of the mind after a gap in time... and here we are talking of five decades. My recurring mental vision of 1950s Berlin is a slow, silent panning shot across a moonscape of endless ruins, still relatively untouched or reconstructed even four years after the war, a desert of broken brick, around Zoo or the Brandenburg Gate, rising and falling in splintered dunes of tumbled city blocks, rolling away to the horizon...and, in the middle of it all, I still see one geriatric truck and trailer with two tiny human figures alongside, lost among the vast destruction, carefully loading up any whole bricks they could find, one by one. After the thousand-year Reich, re-building looked set to be a thousand-year task.

But now, if I add the sounds, I get a more hopeful picture...a tram, jerking and jamming on the tracks, electric sparks spluttering from the wires above...Glenn Miller from a thumb-worn radio on a coffee stall...sausage-sellers, with shiny portable steamers on shoulder straps, mournfully crying their wares ('Heisse Bockwurst, zehn pfennig!').Bronzed and scarred Wehrmacht veterans mending roads and singing about the girl they left behind. And Jeeps!...Jeeps everywhere...British, American, French, throaty and shrill, in high gear, rasping and racehorsing across the cobble stones.

With added sounds, the ruined city comes alive. Women rise up from the cellars with shopping bags. One, in a well-preserved fur coat and feathered hat, is clambering out of a hole in the ground (her home now), stepping over the rubble in her boots but carrying once-smart high heels to wear on the pavement. Incredibly, on the Kurfürstendamm, customers for cherry cheesecake and ice creams are back at the outside tables of the Café Kanzler, watching the world go by. True, there is a severe shortage of young lovers for the violinist to serenade and the mutual smiles of recognition from the pale, elderly survivors soon fade...but they are there, they exist! Even Café des Westens where Rupert Brooke wrote 'Granchester' is just about intact, only a little way from where the broken bricks begin.

From Stettin in the Baltic to Trieste in the Adriatic, an Iron Curtain has descended across the continent.

WINSTON CHURCHILL, MARCH 5TH 1946

Yet at night sometimes, in wakeful moments, I'd hear another sound in desolate isolation... the harsh scream of train wheels on far-off tracks, grinding distantly round uneven bends, a nightmare-ish, human-ish sound that I was told was the result of the welded track the Germans used. To me, though, now that the city really was silent in sleep, it could be a sound screeching out of the collective mouth of the millions who had gone violently to death in these dark, forested lands; sometimes as they desperately fumbled to load a rifle...sometimes as they bent to feed a child...sometimes because they hadn't enough strength inside them to hold on.

Some say the Cold War really began in Britain in the freezing winter of 1947...which is appropriate. I remember it for the way it turned the hills around my home town Stoke-on-Trent into a little Alaska and I joined other sixteen-year-old volunteers to help dig people out of the snow.

At national level it meant that an impoverished Britain was set back even more. One government decision was to cut down on military expenditure and we informed the Americans that we could no longer afford to support the Greek army against the communist armed opposition....whereupon President Truman made the historic decision for the US to take our place and get directly involved, as part of a global attempt to contain the USSR by all means short of all-out war. (The fact that Stalin was not aiding the Greek communists was a detail.)

What it meant was that the Americans were not going home, back into isolation, as after the first world war. So I was to get to meet US servicemen around Berlin, smoke Luckies and Chesterfields and even get invited back to the PX US Army Club for elephant-sized portions of Chicken Maryland and apple pie.

I believe it must be the policy of the United States to support free peoples who are resisting attempted subjugation by armed minorities or outside pressures.

PRESIDENT TRUMAN, MARCH 12TH 1947

Sadly, it also meant that our allies the Red Army were now quietly designated 'the enemy' and them I was not to meet (with one exception, as you'll see). When, in 1950, I became a conscript soldier, the silhouettes of enemies on our firing-range targets had mysteriously been changed from an obvious helmeted German infantryman outline to something unmistakably Russian. Our aristocratic young platoon officer once had us woken at 4am to tell us that Russian paras had landed in peaceful Hampshire and we had to go out and combat them. (As we lurched along nervously in five-ton trucks, one of our number noted that the paper boy was cheerfully doing his rounds, totally untroubled by the red invasion. Maybe he was a fellow traveller...)

But what of the recent enemy? I was fortunate there. Immediately post-war there was an acute shortage of labour on the land. Students like me joined a vast army of temporary workers in 'harvest camps'. An enlightened government invited German students to join us. We were all too young to have fought in the war (though some of them could have been in it at the end). We had a natural curiosity in each other as 'enemies', comparing notes on how the war had affected our teenage lives. Was I too ready to make friends? I know I got criticised for it by people who'd suffered great loss. But, privately, I made up my mind to try and get to Germany when called up.

*

So, like the central character in my play, I was a national serviceman in Berlin in 1950. I more or less went straight from sixth-form into the early days of the Cold War and was to take my place in a world where all those things we were taught not to do at school - lying, cheating, bullying, bringing injury to others - were suddenly found to be absolutely necessary to patriotism, ideological correctness and the fight for freedom.

Not that, as an ordinary soldier, I was required to be any more duplicitous than soldiers tend to be in the normal way of things...no, no, we had spies and secret agents to do the really dirty work for us, didn't we? And they were soon to become the beloved anti-heroes and heroines of the next thirty years, sustaining novel after novel and movie after movie. But, all the same, the corrosion in the hidden channels of our way of life had a way of spreading invisibly just under the surface of our moral metal.

Please don't ever imagine you'll be unscathed by the methods you use. The end may justify the means - if it wasn't supposed to I daresay you wouldn't be here. But there's a price to pay and the price does tend to be oneself.
GEORGE SMILEY TALKING TO TRAINEE SPIES IN *THE SECRET PILGRIM* BY JOHN LE CARRÉ

So Britain allowed young national servicemen to be killed in Malaya (as it was called then) because they could argue that it was the fight against communism, whereas it was a colonial war to keep 'our' rubber and tin. Later Henry Kissinger was to show us in Cambodia that no slaughter of innocents was too great to defend the cause of freedom. (And in Chile that democracy had to be undermined to defend democracy).

But back to Berlin. When I arrived the city was still governed by the Four Power agreement, though it was wearing perilously thin. Germany itself was no longer split into four zones...the Americans, British and French having pooled theirs to set up West Germany as one state. The Russians believed that if we were going to do that then we should give up Berlin, which was deep inside their zone. We refused and issued our newly-created currency into the three western sectors of the city. Russia retaliated by blockading all road and rail routes in and out. The airlift followed, flying everything from potatoes to coal into the city. The Russians gave way (they were losing by it too) and the blockade had just been lifted when I arrived.

Capitalism proceeds not in the path of smooth and even progress but through crisis and the catastrophes of war.
JOSEPH STALIN, FEBRUARY 1946

Which is where I begin my play...Of course there are many autobiographical elements in the story I tell...but it remains a story. I wanted to tell it with an unblinking, unsentimental eye. Too many had suffered; too many had been driven to the edge in trying to put their lives together again and I needed to take account of that. Above all, I was drawn to telling it not because I had some conclusion to offer, but out of my fascination with the power and mystery of human relationships...where characters are tested in their consciences at a time when dishonesty and ruthlessness had been enshrined, both East and West, as an instrument of international policy.

*

I never cease to be astonished at the speed with which the communist world seemed to vanish in all its outward signs and icons...the gleaming stars, the monster slogans, the snapping banners, all gone...I might say 'with the wind'. Maybe, as with the Confederate South, a sentimental preservation industry will grow up to keep the memory alive. Maybe not...

The icons may have been removed but the Cold War still continues. The moving of the borders of NATO eastwards into Poland, Hungary and the Czech Republic drives a wedge between Russia and Europe that bodes ill for the future. Has the moment gone when Russia wanted to talk about association with Europe? Does the US agenda weigh against it? As a playwright I want a playwright's Europe and that must include the land of Gogol, Turgenev and Chekhov.

So there is no way I can, or would, want to feel remotely nostalgic about those self-destructive times that still won't let us go. Even as I write this, espionage is back in the news in the US and in Moscow. Do we always have to have 'the enemy'? Are we biologically pre-set to be so easily brainwashed into mindless tribal hostility?

I don't think we are. I think, individually, we can control it. The trouble is we let those who think otherwise control us.

Peter Whelan, London, March 2001

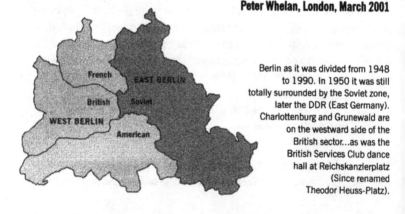

Berlin as it was divided from 1948 to 1990. In 1950 it was still totally surrounded by the Soviet zone, later the DDR (East Germany). Charlottenburg and Grunewald are on the westward side of the British sector...as was the British Services Club dance hall at Reichskanzlerplatz (Since renamed Theodor Heuss-Platz).

A Russian in the Woods

A Russian in the Woods was first performed at RSC The Other Place, Stratford, on 21 March 2001. The cast was as follows:

Pat Harford	Anthony Flanagan
Clive Burns	Colin Mace
Sergeant Dilke	Stuart Goodwin
Captain Geoff Wirral	Charlie Simpson
Ilse Bucher	Anna Madeley
Fraser Cullen	Louis Hilyer
Dieter Stahl	David Hinton
Corporal Lloyd Jackson	Douglas Rao

Directed by Robert Delamere
Designed by Simon Higlett
Lighting by Rick Fisher
Music by Harry Peat

Act One

Scene One

Germany, near Hanover, summer of 1950, midday.

A bench by the wire of a tennis court at a British Army barracks. The actor playing **Pat Harford** *narrates the story as though he has heard it from his character's present-day self. He wears crumpled, borrowed tennis whites and is sweaty and dusty from a game just finished.*

His sergeant's 'shirtsleeve order' uniform (summer wear: no jacket, sleeves rolled up) with blue beret, webbing belt and gaiters, is draped over the bench (cap badge of the RAEC . . . Royal Army Educational Corps). His borrowed racket and a scuffed sports bag are beside him.

On the wire behind him is a notice, a Union Jack top left and the Berlin insignia (black disc surrounded by red ring) top right. It reads: Service personnel and guests only.

Pat He said . . . (*Pauses.*) He said this all began with something that has stayed in his mind sharply for over fifty years . . . that unexpected . . . *uncanny* game of tennis. He said the game itself wasn't worth remembering . . . what did he call it? 'A left-footed knock-up with scoring'. But it was the situation. He played it at an almost deserted British Army base near Hanover, the day before he got to Berlin. We're talking of 1950, four years after the war . . . and not long after the Berlin Airlift. The Russians, who surrounded the city, had re-opened the road and rail routes . . . and Sergeant Pat Harford (*Indicates himself.*), national serviceman, fresh from England, was on his way there. He was nineteen . . . experiencing things back then in the way that I do now, as I talk to you and tell you that, today, he's touching seventy.

He thinks about this before resuming the story:

He'd arrived at this ex-Wehrmacht barracks with three hundred other British conscripts but they'd all left by the end of the morning, posted to various parts of Germany. As he was the only one travelling to Berlin he had to wait for the midnight train and had twelve hours to kill. He took a silent walk among the sun-drenched barrack blocks and one-time parade grounds of the Third Reich . . . and, suddenly, found himself, of all places, by the tennis courts. There were a dozen of them, built in Hitler's time; a wide red desert with sharp etched lines, and no sign of life . . . except that, at the moment, he felt a presence alongside him . . .

Clive Burns *appears, dressed in tennis whites. He's an overweight, unhealthy-looking man, some ten years older than* **Pat***.*

And there the man was . . . the only other living soul in this place of spirits. It was as though he'd appeared out of the air, in his whites, like a ghost at midday. He offered Pat a racket and kit and shouted . . .

Clive   Hello there! D'you play?

The actor playing **Pat** *doesn't immediately answer, or acknowledge him. At the moment* **Clive** *is only a character remembered in the story the actual* **Pat** *had told.*

Pat   Pat said it caught him totally on the wrong foot . . . He didn't particularly want to. He wasn't in the mood to . . . but he found himself saying:

Without looking at **Clive***, as though remembering,* **Pat** *says:*

Yes, I play. Not that well . . . but I play.

It's still a story. **Clive** *doesn't move.*

So, that's how it started. In the heat of that long departed day, in badly fitting kit, with a dodgy racket, against an opponent who never gave his name, or his rank, Pat played two sets . . . and lost both.

Immediately we are in real time. The two men start vigorous towelling, as though they've just come off the courts. Presently **Clive** *speaks.*

Clive   Good! That's got me going. Play another?

Pat   You're joking.

Clive *puts his racket in a frame and a clutch of balls in the bag.*

Clive   Too hot for you?

Pat   Soaked. Why do I sweat so much?

Clive   Sweat's good for you. When you've been over here a while you'll have that inside you you'll want to sweat out. Still, I'm sorry to get you on court at noon. The only time I can manage. But I prefer the sun overhead . . . no shadows . . . everything's clear. The same with a room . . . I can't stand low-level lighting. Give me one bright bulb in the middle of the ceiling. I don't like shadows. (*Looks in bag.*) Another ball somewhere . . .

Peers about. So does **Pat**. **Clive** *spots it.*

I see it. Stay where you are, Sergeant.

He exits. The actor playing **Pat** *speaks to audience.*

Pat   Pat said he was convinced the man was an officer . . . even if he didn't seem like one. What the hell! It was all ludicrous. He felt it enough of a farce being a sergeant at his age. All he was was a civilian in uniform. He'd been made a sergeant instructor in the Royal Army Educational Corps. Literally, he'd become a schoolteacher, even though he was straight from sixth form. He was to teach general knowledge to soldiers, some of them twice his age. All troops now had to undergo compulsory education, which was not received with universal joy. You got the three stripes for protection, not merit.

Clive *returns and puts the stray ball in the bag.*

Clive   Know who these courts were made for originally?

Pat   Who?

Clive   The Waffen SS. This was their barracks.

Pat   Funny to think of the SS playing tennis . . .

Clive   You didn't argue line decisions.

Pat *removes his tennis shoes and hands them over.*

Pat   Thanks for the shoes.

Clive   Did they fit?

Pat   Fine. I'm not blaming them.

Clive   Hard to get in Germany just now. They have a way of walking.

He takes the shoes and puts them in the bag.

I used to carry three sizes . . . now I'm down to two. And, of course, I never know what size feet my opponent's going to have, do I?

Pat   D'you always find someone to play?

Clive   Usually. It's a coming-and-going sort of place, this. There's generally someone on their way from here to there who plays. Like you.

Pat *beats dust from his shirt.*

Pat   Did you notice the dust?

Clive   What dust?

Pat   Red dust in the air, over the courts. I've got it on your shirt, I'm sorry.

Clive   It's red ash. Haven't you played red ash before?

Pat   No.

Clive   Good surface. Nothing but the best for the SS.

Pat   Gets in your eyes . . .

Clive   You were kicking it up more than I was.

Pat   No. I mean . . . it was there before we started playing. Did you notice? When I looked up to serve I could see it in the air . . . all this sharp red dust . . . as though it was blown there . . .

Clive   There's no wind.

Pat (*uncertain*)   I was going to say . . . no wind.

A moment. **Pat** *feels slightly foolish.*

Clive   What did you play on, back home? Grass?

Pat (*amused*)   Grass? No, what d'you call it? Black asphalt. It's all they had round our way, even in the park.

Clive   You learned in the park?

Pat   Yes.

Clive   Not school?

Pat   Boys school. Didn't do tennis.

Clive   So you went to the park.

Pat   Yes.

Clive   Where the girls were?

Pat   Yes.

Clive   Foursomes . . .

Pat   Yes.

Clive   Twosomes . . .

Pat   Sometimes . . .

Clive   Who taught you your service?

Pat (*edgy*)   I did.

Clive *leaves it.* **Pat** *gets out of the shorts.*

Clive   I'm sorry about the shorts. They belonged to a friend of mine. He was a bit of a strange shape. Anyway, he got himself out.

Pat   Demobbed?

Clive   He died.

Pat   I'm sorry. In the war?

Clive   No. His liver. He should have sweated more.

Pat *becomes self-conscious as he gets into his army trousers and then removes tennis shirt.*

Clive   Would you like me to tell you why you lost?

Pat   Because I'm not good enough.

Clive   You lost because you didn't want to win.

Pat   Course I wanted to win.

Clive   Not enough.

Pat   I think I'd know about that, wouldn't I?

Clive   You have some good strokes. I don't have the strokes. You're fitter than me. Faster. But you let me win. Not at first. You started well. Played a blinder. Good smash . . . backhand volley. You came at me from everywhere. I said to you, d'you remember? . . . 'Is this your usual game?' You didn't say anything . . . but you laughed. You just laughed. Remember it? A little laugh . . . didn't you? And in that laugh I caught a certain tone. It told me you didn't really care about winning.

Pat   It was just a laugh.

Clive   No . . .

Pat   It struck me as ironic.

Clive   What did?

Pat   You come to Germany expecting some kind of nightmare.

Clive   Do you?

Pat   The destruction . . . everything in pieces. Instead, here I am on a tennis court on a bright summer's day being asked: 'Is this your usual game?' It's ironic.

Clive   I'll tell you one thing about tennis. You can't play it ironically.

Pat No?

Clive No. You either win or you lose.

Pat Oh, I expect you're right. Yes, that would be the case. Win or lose. Yes.

Clive (*ignoring the sarcasm*)   I'm what would be called a boring player. No, no . . . I accept it. Boring. And once I saw that you didn't want to win I played even more boring. Stayed back. Retrieved. Kept a plodding length and let you beat yourself. I ground you down, Sergeant.

Pat *is stopped by the use of his rank.*

Pat Should I be calling you 'sir'?

Clive Am I wearing any insignia of rank?

Pat No.

Clive Then don't call me anything. What I'm saying is: you were in a position of strength. Look at me! Too many late nights . . . too many dawns . . . too many smoke-filled bars. A travesty of the human condition. Now look at you . . . fresh from a hundred hours of square-bashing. Fit as a flea. So . . . the difference has to be here . . .

Taps his head.

The brain. The will. You had the triumph of the body but not of the will!

Pat What's that mean?

Clive Everything, if you're going to win!

Pat It's for enjoyment!

Clive It's what?

Pat To enjoy!

Clive Say again . . .

Pat It's a game!

Clive It's war! It's war carried on by other means. It's like the war we have here.

Pat What war?

Clive What war? (*Then:*) Why were you hanging about doing sweet fuck-all when I asked you to play?

Pat Got to wait for my train.

Clive Because you volunteered for Berlin.

Pat How d'you know I volunteered?

Clive You're an education sergeant. Everyone in your outfit who goes to Berlin garrison volunteers. Maybe you like the idea of being surrounded . . .

Pat I like the idea of seeing something for myself. Berlin's where it's happening.

Clive The 'epicentre'.

Pat As they say . . .

Clive And that's educational . . .

Pat Right.

Clive But why should you have to wait for the midnight train?

Pat Because it's the only train to Berlin.

Clive Why? Why don't they do us a favour and run a daytime train?

Pat Because the Soviets won't allow it.

Clive Oh, is that why?

Pat I think so . . .

Clive All right. Why would the Soviets insist that we travel at night?

Pat The line goes through their zone. They don't want us to see their positions.

Clive   We know their positions. And they know we know. Our agreement says they must let us through. They say: All right you can go through . . . but only in the dark. That's psychological. They want to put the fear of Lenin up you. Through the night to the forbidden city that they want you to think of as their territory . . . so you do it on their terms. It's called the cold war. I prefer 'calculated war'. A thinking war, like our game. They send shots from every angle. We have to think of a way of getting them back . . . or lose. Did you know you have to keep the blinds down all the way to Berlin?

Pat (*alarmed*)   No . . .

Clive   All the way to Charlottenburg station. All window blinds fastened in place. Regulations.

Pat   So I won't see any Russians?

Clive   D'you want to?

Pat   I'm just curious.

Clive   Know your enemy?

He sees **Pat** *objects to defining the Russians as the enemy.*

What you do is what everyone else does. You lift up the corner of the blind and peep out. They know we do it; they want us to do it, because by doing it they've forced us to grovel. Take a peek out at around six tomorrow morning and you'll see all the Russians you want.

By now **Pat** *has his uniform on and all the kit he borrowed is in* **Clive**'s *bag.*

Thanks for the game.

Pat   Thanks for the kit.

Clive   You'll be cooler in Berlin. You've got the lakes. Go to the army sports ground when you're there, next to the Olympic Stadium. There's a tennis professional called

Gerhart. He'll sort out your service. Play to win, Sergeant. Good luck.

Pat *lets him go.*

Pat   Up yours . . . sir.

Fade to black.

Scene Two

Hanover station, military area, Berlin platform. A redcap military police sergeant, **Sergeant Dilke**, *stands waiting to check departing personnel. We hear background announcements in German for civilians on other platforms and in English for BAOR forces.*

Pat *appears, now in full battledress (battle blouse jacket and tie; large and small packs on back, a kitbag on his shoulder and a personal-belongings suitcase in his hand). He gets out his papers and checks in with* **Sergeant Dilke**.

Pat   Berlin?

Dilke (*sharply*)   Sergeant, Sergeant!

Pat is thrown for a moment. What **Dilke** *means is that he insists on being addressed as sergeant, even though they are both sergeants. This is ultra 'regimental' and not uncommon with redcaps.*

Pat (*correcting*)   Berlin, Sergeant?

Dilke   Name, Sergeant?

Pat   Harford, Sergeant.

Pat hands over papers. **Dilke** *checks his clipboard.*

Dilke   Two double oh nine eight three six, Sergeant?

Pat   No, Sergeant.

Pat knows the sergeant has changed one digit as a security test. He finds this tiresome and stays silent, forcing **Dilke** *to speak first.*

Dilke (*quietly*)   So correct me.

Pat   Two double oh nine seven three six.

Dilke *doesn't bother to acknowledge that this is correct.*

Dilke   You're in D5, Sergeant. You have a sleeping compartment to yourself so there won't be anyone to ask anything of, so ask me now if there's something you're not sure about. Have you read the regulations?

Pat (*warily*)   Yes, Sergeant.

Dilke   Once you are in your compartment? . . .

Pat   Stay put.

Dilke   Do not, repeat not, move about the train unless ordered to do so. What about window blinds?

Pat   Keep them down.

Dilke   And if the Russians climb aboard in the middle of the night and point their nasty weapons at you, what do you say?

Pat (*off guard*)   I don't know . . .

Dilke   You say: '*Ya sdayoos.*'

Pat   What's that?

Dilke   It means: 'I surrender.'

It dawns on **Pat** *that this is meant to be a joke.*

Smile at them. Give name, rank and number. That's all. What we're saying is do not try to be a hero unless requested to be so by a superior officer. The problem with posthumous medals for heroism is that you'd never know you'd been given one, would you, Sergeant?

Pat   What was it again?

Dilke   *Ya sdayoos.*

Pat   *Ya sdayoos?*

Dilke   Correct.

Dilke *waves him on through the steam of the platform.*

Blackout.

Scene Three

On the train **Pat** *has found his sleeper and dumps his kitbag and case. He gazes about him.*

Pat   Pat had never been in a sleeper before. Come to that, he'd never travelled first class before. He says you have to imagine the effect on someone of his background, coming from a land of post-war austerity . . . to find himself in a first-class 1930s German sleeping car with all the trimmings. It was well worn and faded but definitely the real thing: polished wood, leather, linen, silk cords, starched cotton, silver-plated taps and bevelled mirrors, casting tiny rainbow lights. It was a world that had disappeared down another track, long ago, but the British had commandeered it, even for their sergeants. Such are the spoils of war . . .

The steam loco gets slowly under way, creaking eerily. **Pat** *takes off his jacket and rummages in his case for pyjamas and washbag, then sits, mesmerised by his situation. He peeps round the blind, sees nothing and lies on the bed.*

All he could see round the edge of the blind was solid darkness. He says he didn't expect to sleep but, somewhere past one thirty, he floated into a swaying dream as the train, sighing and booming like a whale, swam out of Saxony, past Wolfsburg to the frontier and into the wide night-time sea of the Soviet zone.

The sleeper's lights have clicked out leaving only a dim blue nightlight. **Pat** *is dozing. The first grey light of dawn sways in from outside as the train slows. He wakes suddenly . . . remembers where he is and goes for the window blind.*

Soon after dawn he peeped out. There, as the man said, drenched in grey fog, was a Soviet army base. Its wire was right by the track, its huts within throwing distance. More of it and more of it, rolling on as the train crept by. Lorries, troop carriers, artillery . . . and tanks! T34s, scores of them, parked by the barrack blocks. They had caked earth on their tracks . . . their turret guns were angled down, as though in sleep.

The sound of Red Army men singing 'Kalinka', very faintly at first, then gradually stronger.

Then he saw brown smudges in the mist . . . stretching arms . . . yawning . . . heading for washrooms . . . lining up for breakfast . . . the Red Army! Our doppelgänger. Our other selves. And so close he could have called out 'Tovarich!'

Scene Four

Five weeks later, Friday afternoon, the admin room of an army education centre in Charlottenburg, the elegant western district of Berlin. The room was once one of the reception rooms of a spacious nineteenth-century villa. It has imposing doors to the hall and equally imposing glass doors to the neglected terrace and ornamental garden, the latter small compared with the size of the house, which is fairly close to its neighbours (as large villas are in Kensington). The house beyond the garden has fared worse in the war. Hit by Soviet artillery, it is a gaping ruin.

Little of the original furniture of the room remains. The army has kitted it out with a secretarial desk, with phone and typewriter, a trestle table, file cabinet, assorted chairs and a noticeboard for educational publicity, lists of army units, classes, timetable, part one orders, part two orders, fire regulations, etc.

Two items are not normally in the room: a 16-mil cinema projector in the background and, dumped in the foreground, a German army iron barrack bed, scuffed and a bit rusty, with a mattress rolled up, tied with rope, plus pillow, blankets and sheets in a folded bundle.

Captain Geoff Wirral *enters, booted and gaitered for travel, a holdall in hand. He looks in the file for papers, then notices the bed with distaste.*

Geoff *(calls out)* Who sent this bed? Ilse! Who sent it?

Enter **Ilse** *with a briefcase, which she hands to him.*

Who sent this suppurating, scrofulous bed?

Ilse Stores.

Geoff Yes . . . stores. But who? Sergeant McKay?

Ilse He's on leave.

Geoff *(remembers something he might need)* The manual in here?

Checks briefcase.

Ilse Yes.

Geoff The amendments?

Ilse Everything you ask. Nothing is missing.

He resents her tone. Returns to the subject of the bed.

Geoff Who sent it? The bed?

Ilse Corporal Stott.

Geoff Sod Stott! This is a clapped-out, confiscated ex-Wehrmacht cast-off and I don't want it on my territory.

Ilse It's fine.

Geoff We'll be lucky if someone hasn't had dysentery in it.

Ilse It's been disinfected.

Geoff Smells of formaldehyde and cheese. Get Stott on the phone.

Ilse Oh God!

Geoff   And don't despise me more than you normally despise me. Your everyday tone of weary disgust is more than adequate. Where's Fraser?

Ilse   Garden.

She goes to phone. **Geoff** *calls to garden.*

Geoff   Staff Sergeant Cullen!

Fraser Cullen *enters, very dapper in flannels and dark blue, double-breasted blazer.*

Fraser   Sir!

Geoff   Don't you ever wear uniform?

Fraser   Oh, that's not fair, sir. Not on duty till eighteen hundred.

Ilse (*on phone*)   Education Centre, Charlottenburg, Corporal Stott please.

Fraser   I am here in my own free time.

Ilse (*on phone*)   Captain Wirral wants to speak to him . . . (*Waits.*)

Geoff (*despairing*)   Your cufflinks!

Fraser   Dutch. Bit naughty. Got them in Amsterdam. Gold testicles.

Ilse (*on phone*)   Thank you. (*Puts phone down.*) Back in half an hour.

Geoff (*to* **Ilse**)   He's there!

Ilse   They say not.

Geoff   If there's one thing worse than dumb insolence it's telephonic insolence. We're just a joke in this army. Education Corps? Anything'll do for us. If we were Eleventh Hussars or Black Watch . . . or, God help us, even the King's Own Liverpools we wouldn't be sent such rubbish. One of our sergeants has to sleep on this!

Fraser   Not bad. It's got sheets. There were times in the desert I used to dream about sheets.

Geoff   Let me tell you what's happening this weekend . . .

Ilse   I told him.

Geoff (*ignoring her*)   I'm taking the staff to Hanover on an update course and the Education Centre is closed till Tuesday. I asked Ilse to get you round . . .

Ilse   I told him . . .

Geoff (*ignoring*)   . . . to take away your projector. It's Army Kinema Corps property; you are Army Kinema Corps, so you should take responsibility.

Fraser   And here I am to take it away, sir.

Geoff   You don't look dressed for moving a projector.

Fraser   I'm not sure how you would dress for moving a projector.

Geoff   We were burgled last time the place was empty. Major Rogers has decided that we should have an Ed Corps presence . . . especially with what's in the garden . . . so he's sending a sergeant that he doesn't know what else to do with to sleep here and keep an eye on it. Forgets, of course, that there aren't any beds here . . . so I sent for one and got this.

Gives it a weary look.

They said, after the war, the world would be a better place.

Fraser   It will be, sir. It will be.

Geoff   I'm tired of being on the receiving end. Bad enough being condemned to a long weekend of boredom on this Hanover thing. Some smart-arsed staff officers constructing so-called educational theory out of what our common sense told us years ago . . . taking that which was once obvious and practical and rendering it utterly obscure and useless! I am worn out with losing, Fraser, I really am.

Having directed some of this at **Ilse**, *he exits to the hall.*

Fraser (*sighs*)   Yo-ho-ho. He wouldn't be in the doghouse again would he?

Ilse   Yes.

Fraser *sweeps her up in an embrace and kisses her.*

Fraser   *Liebling, Liebling!* Are you sure you know what the doghouse is?

Ilse   Yes. When a wife is making trouble.

Fraser   And is she?

Ilse   Yes! I'm saying this!

Fraser   About what?

Ilse   Me.

Fraser   What have you been doing?

Ilse   Nothing!

Fraser   And she still thinks? . . .

Ilse   Think! She doesn't think.

Fraser   She won't do anything, *Liebling.*

Ilse   I could lose this job.

Fraser   She won't do anything.

Ilse   The bitch.

Fraser   She won't. She knows it's all over. It is all over, isn't it?

Ilse   Yes. Which is what makes him the more angry.

Fraser   Maybe he'll have fun in Hanover.

Ilse (*amused*)   Maybe.

Fraser   Perhaps I should lend him my address book . . .

He begins to ease her black mood by singing a German version of 'Is You Is Or Is You Ain't My Baby'. **Fraser** *sings it very softly, so it won't be heard by* **Geoff**. *He draws her into a jiving, jitterbugging dance . . . keeping the noise down so* **Geoff** *doesn't hear.*

> *Bist du bist oder bist du nicht mein Baby? . . .*
> *Dein Benehmen macht mich fühlen blue.*
> *Bist du bist oder bist du nicht mein Baby?*
> *Oder geht mein Baby aus mit jemand new?*

Ilse *is too upset to join in the mood of it.*

Ilse   No . . . I am not funny!

Fraser   *Mein Baby! Bist du nicht?*

Ilse   I'm not feeling funny, Fraser!

Enter **Pat**, *hesitantly, with suitcase.* **Ilse** *stops dancing.* **Fraser** *continues solo.*

Fraser   Good afternoon, Sergeant!

Pat   Afternoon, sir.

Fraser   Not 'sir' . . . 'Staff'.

Pat   Staff. I'm Sergeant Harford, Staff. A bit late. I'm sorry . . .

Fraser   No, just in time for dance classes. How's your jitterbug?

Pat   Never done it . . .

Fraser   Never? What are they teaching you in basic training these days? With me!

Pat *makes some vague movements in response.*

Ilse (*to* **Pat**)   You told the driver to wait?

Pat   Yes. He said he's taking Captain Wirral.

Ilse   I'll check.

She exits to hall.

Fraser   I'm Staff Sergeant Fraser Cullen, Army Kinema Corps. I'm assistant manager at the garrison cinema.

Pat   At Reichskanzlerplatz?

Fraser   The same.

Pat   I went last Thursday . . . I saw *Born Yesterday*.

Fraser   Judy Holliday! Wow!

Pat   Yes, wow!

Fraser   Wow, wow, wow! What a voice!

Pat (*attempt at Bronx accent*)   Woudja do me a favour, Harry . . . dwap dead!

Fraser (*imitates*)   And as far as I'm consoined . . . vice voica!

Enter **Geoff** *with* **Ilse**. **Pat** *salutes,* **Geoff** *aknowledges with a curt nod.*

Geoff   You're late, Sergeant.

Pat   The driver went astray, sir.

Geoff (*to* **Pat**)   I hear you've been in Berlin five weeks and they still haven't found you a posting. What have you been doing?

Pat   General duties, sir . . .

Geoff   At ease, Sergeant. Hat off.

Pat   And seeing the city.

Fraser   We all do that sometimes.

Geoff   We're sorry to interrupt your happy holiday with this terrible chore, stuck here for the weekend. But I've won permission from Major Rogers for you to take two hours off for dinner at the mess each evening.

Pat   Thank you, sir.

Geoff   Can't have you going round the twist.

Pat   No, sir.

Geoff   There's no real reason for you to be here, you do appreciate? There's absolutely nothing to do.

Fraser   That's right, sir. Make him feel wanted.

Geoff   So, you can sit and improve your mind. Got any reading matter?

Pat   Sir . . .

He fishes two paperbacks from the pocket of the case then instantly regrets it.

Geoff   Anything interesting?

Pat   Oh . . . it's er . . . a novel. *Fathers and Sons.*

Geoff   The Russian novel?

Pat (*nods, slightly nervous*)   Yes, sir. Turgenev. And some short stories . . . (*pause*) by Chekhov.

Geoff   Also Russian.

This hangs in the air a moment.

Pat   My father gave them to me . . . (*as though explaining*) *Fathers and Sons.*

Geoff   Good. I hope you get something out of being here. Nice garden to relax in. Bit overgrown.

Pat   It's a beautiful house, sir. I've not been in Charlottenburg before. You'd hardly know there'd been a war. All these villas and trees. They seem untouched.

Geoff   You should look a bit harder, Sergeant. There's bullet holes front and back and our neighbour over there took two direct hits from Russian artillery. May not have been flattened like the city centre but this was the scene of the last battle for Berlin, wasn't it, Staff?

Fraser   Down the road you've got Spandau and Ruhleben. That's where you had Hitler Youth . . . twelve- and fourteen-year-olds, against Zhukov's tank divisions.

Geoff *knows this distresses* **Ilse**, *so he lays it on.*

Geoff   And German panzers desperate to escape west to surrender to the Americans instead of the Soviets. They panicked and ran over the refugees on Charlottenburg bridge. Eyewitnesses report gobbets of human flesh bobbing about downriver for days.

This is to provoke **Ilse**'s *sensibilities. She makes for the door.*

Ilse   OK. I'll find things to do.

Geoff   I'll need the exhumation letter!

This stops her leaving. She finds it in the file.

Fraser   Nice to be able to say that, isn't it? 'I'll need the exhumation letter.'

Geoff (*to* **Pat**)   Major Rogers tell you about the exhumation?

Pat (*puzzled*)   No, sir.

Geoff   There may be a couple of corpses buried in the far corner of the garden. He didn't mention it?

Pat   No, sir. I'd have remembered.

Geoff *shows him the letter.*

Geoff   Two German soldiers buried in the last days of the siege. A prisoner of war back from Russia said he recalled helping to bury them in this garden. That was in April '45. He only got repatriated a month ago; the Russians take their time . . . Anyway, we didn't know till last week when he came round and told us. You see the area in the corner marked with tapes?

Pat *looks where he is indicating through the garden doors.*

Pat   Yes . . .

Geoff   Under there.

Fraser   Corpses keep turning up all over the city. They found six in a row under a hotel car park in Tiergarten last week.

Geoff   The army deal with the Berlin authorities over it. Nothing will happen while you're here . . . but, no one's allowed in that corner for any reason whatever and anyone asking about it you refer them to Army Burials . . . number's here. (*Refers to letter.*)

Pat   Who might ask about it?

Ilse   He means mothers or wives. No one important.

Geoff *ignores her sarcasm and shows him a list of phone numbers.*

Geoff   Military police number for emergencies. And this one's the Nightwatch Security Service . . . have you come across them?

Pat   No, sir . . .

Geoff   German civilian personnel employed by us to keep an eye on unguarded military establishments. They normally do spot checks on this place from twenty-three hundred on. If you fall ill and have to leave the house overnight, ring them on this one . . . after you've reported the matter to Major Rogers, of course . . .

He gives him a searching glance, as though **Pat** *and the major might have some other agenda going. He then finishes going through the list.*

Other useful numbers. This in case of fire . . . d'you smoke?

Pat   Trying to give up, sir.

Geoff   Good. Now . . . sleeping . . . Upstairs is more or less gutted . . . we don't use it. Just bare rooms and no bloody lights, I'm afraid . . . the circuit keeps shorting out. A thousand unemployed electricians walking the streets of West Berlin and can we get it seen to? . . . can we buggery, because we have to do it through army maintenance . . . so I suggest you sleep down here. Well, in any case, you're nearer the phone here.

Fraser   Now you're making me nervous.

Geoff   Sergeant Harford's not nervous.

Pat   No, sir. Not yet.

Geoff   You may be when you try the bed, which Ilse accepted delivery of despite its evil condition.

Pat *'rescues'* **Ilse**.

Pat   Seems OK.

Geoff   Looks as though it came out of a mortuary.

Pat   I didn't know they had beds in mortuaries . . .

Fraser *and* **Ilse** *amused. For* **Geoff** *it only confirms, like the Russian books, that this sergeant should be watched.*

Fraser   He has a point there, sir.

Geoff   Ye-e-ss. Well, if you're prepared to put up with it, good. Get ready, Ilse . . . I'll drop you off at the station.

Ilse   I have the things to collect.

Geoff   Then collect them. We can't have Sergeant Harford distracted by you. He'll have a hard enough job getting Staff Cullen to remove his projector.

Ilse, *reluctantly, collects items.*

Fraser   It will be done, sir.

Geoff   Oh, come on, Fraser. You just want to hang about beguiling the sergeant with your anecdotes.

Fraser   No beguiling, sir, I promise.

Geoff *gets logbook for* **Pat**.

Geoff   Logbook. Enter anything of note and specifically anyone arriving or (*to* **Fraser**) departing. (*To* **Ilse**.) Keys?

Ilse (*bringing them*)   Front door, these two. This is the garden door. They're all labelled. (*To* **Geoff**.) He hasn't signed the inventory.

Geoff   No time. Fraser can take him through it.

Ilse   Fraser doesn't know where the items are. I will stay.

Geoff   Don't mess me about! You're getting in that car . . . now!

A moment of tension as **Ilse** *almost rebels . . . then she flings down the inventory clipboard, grabs her things and exits to the hall.* **Geoff** *is quietly satisfied.*

Do it properly, Sergeant.

Pat   Sir.

Geoff   I've no doubt Major Rogers will want a report from you . . .

Pat   He didn't say so, sir.

Geoff (*not convinced*)   Didn't he? See you Tuesday a.m. (*Indicates the projector.*) Staff Sergeant Cullen . . . your responsibility.

He exits to the hall before **Fraser** *can reply.*

Fraser   Thank you, sir.

Sound of car departing. **Fraser** *listens and makes sure* **Geoff** *is gone.*

Pat   What's going on, Staff?

Fraser   He thinks Major Rogers has sent you to spy on him, doesn't he?

Pat   Me?

Fraser   Hasn't he?

Pat   No. Why should he?

Fraser   Because Geoffrey's not the major's favourite officer, just now.

Pat *waits for him to say why but he doesn't.*

Pat   What I'm really asking is . . . why's he treat her like that?

Fraser   Can't you tell?

Pat *shakes his head.*

Fraser   She stopped letting him into her knickers.

Now **Pat** *is embarrassed.*

Pat *(taken aback)*   Yes . . . well.

Fraser   She got tired of being blackmailed. Her job depends on him, doesn't it? He was expecting her to do a regular turn if she wanted to carry on working. Came the time she said no.

Pat   What did he do?

Fraser   Turned nasty. He thinks he has a God-given right to get his end away. He'd shag the regimental goat if it wasn't so choosy.

Pat *lets that bounce off him, still thinking seriously about* **Ilse**.

Pat   He shouldn't have spoken to her like that.

Fraser   Like what?

Pat   Making her go.

Fraser   Did you want her to stay?

Pat   She didn't want to go!

Fraser *appraises his feelings for* **Ilse**. *Then:*

Fraser   This projector. I lent it to the centre as a favour so they could show 35-mil film. All they have issued here is 16-mil. It's due to me that they can show movies instead of their 16-mil training rubbish. They'll need it again on

Wednesday! It's a bit of a sod, taking it away and bringing it back.

Pat   I didn't know there was an Army Kinema Corps.

Fraser   The AKC? Not many do. Well, we were a very closely guarded secret when we were formed. That was in the Western Desert in 1942. We were raised to help defeat Rommel's Afrika Korps at the Battle of El Alamein. What we did was mount enormous, specially constructed cinema screens on the front of our tanks. These were driven steadily towards the enemy while the AKC drove behind projecting on to those screens a series of pornographic movies shot in the back streets of Cairo. The Germans saw them and were instantly depraved and corrupted and lost the will to fight. As Montgomery said, 'Even the most highly twained soldier cannot pwoperly aim a wifle and wank simultaneously . . . '

Pat savours the thought.

Pat   Why do we never get the truth about these things?

Fraser   Churchill had to suppress it, didn't he? If we'd gone on like that we'd have won the war in six months . . . but he'd promised us blood, toil, tears and sweat . . . so blood, toil, tears and sweat it had to be.

He inwardly recalls the grimness of it.

Pat   Were you really in it in the war?

Fraser   I was in the Seventh Armoured . . . one of the original Desert Rats, my son! All the way from Egypt to the Rhine. I should have got demobbed and gone home but you can't go home if you haven't got one, can you? The army's my home. I was once a projectionist in Brighton for three weeks before the war. On the strength of that I signed on again with the AKC. I love cushy numbers . . . mind you, you're not doing so badly . . . nice sunny weekend in the garden . . .

Pat   I wasn't expecting two corpses to be in it.

Fraser   I don't suppose they were. Has he listed them?

Pat *searches the itinerary.*

Pat   No.

Fraser   So you don't have to account for them.

Pat   Well, this is a list of property. A body isn't anyone's property, strictly speaking.

Fraser   Not when there's no one inside it.

Pat   But how would you know there's no one inside it?

Fraser   You ask.

Re-enter **Ilse** *in a rage.*

Ilse   He's a shit!

Fraser   *Liebling! Was ist los?*

Ilse   At the station . . . I get out of the car. He shouts through the window, 'Go home scrubber!' People there can hear this. His driver can hear. 'Go home, scrubber!'

Fraser   He wouldn't know what it meant.

Ilse   Anyone who knows the British knows what 'scrubber' means. Fuck him!

Fraser   Now . . . English ladies don't say that.

Ilse   Fuck English ladies!

Pat   Hear, hear!

Ilse (*to* **Fraser**, *indicating* **Pat**)   Does he laugh at me?

Pat   No.

Fraser (*to* **Ilse**)   Come here.

He embraces her.

Oh, *Liebling . . . mein Schatz . . . mein Blümchen . . .* what shall we do with you?

Ilse   To hell with this job!

Fraser   No, be sensible. You're not being sensible . . .

Ilse   *Es ist unmöglich!*

Fraser   We don't want Geoffrey knowing you came back, do we? Let's say you came back for something you forgot . . . Then the sergeant won't have to put it in his log.

He says this for **Pat**'s *benefit.*

Pat   I won't enter it.

Ilse   I came back to leave him a note saying I resign.

Fraser   No.

Ilse   Yes!

Fraser   You can't afford to.

Ilse   I shall get a job with the Americans.

Fraser   Everyone wants a job with the Americans.

Ilse   Shut up!

Fraser   Come on . . . you're upsetting Pat. He's on your side. He was very angry at the way Geoff treated you. Now! Pat's the one to teach you American. (*To* **Pat**.) She wants coaching in American accent.

Pat   Why?

Fraser   She thinks it'll increase her earning potential. Speak some American.

Pat   You're better at it than me.

Fraser   Not me . . . you. Do your Judy Holliday. Go on . . .

Pat   I can't do it cold . . .

Fraser   Yes you can. He does a lovely Judy Holliday . . . Just for Ilse.

Pat (*Brooklyn*)   Wouldja do me a favour, Harry . . . dwap dead!

Fraser   See!

Ilse (*doubtful*)   Is that good American?

Pat   Well . . . sort of Bronx American . . .

Ilse   Bronx? Is that good?

Fraser   The best. You listen to him. This is an educated boy. Now . . . there should be three bottles of red in the kitchen. Has he listed them? Shouldn't have. I brought them.

Ilse   He has.

Fraser (*checks list*)   Bloody hell!

Ilse   You gave them to him, you creeper!

Fraser (*correcting*)   Creep. 'Creepers' climb up walls. Creeps only brown-nose.

Ilse   Creep.

Fraser   That's better.

Ilse (*more insulting*)   Creep!

Fraser   We'll open one bottle, at any rate. I'll replace it.

Ilse   Creep!

He exits to hall. **Ilse** *turns to* **Pat**.

Red, red . . . (*The wine has reminded her.*) How d'you say 'red'?

Pat (*thinking she means in English*)   Red.

Ilse   No . . . in American! Like 'When the red, red robin comes bob, bob bobbing along'?

Pat   They say red like we say red.

Ilse   You sure?

Pat   'Red, red robin . . .' No . . . that's Irish. 'When the red, red robin . . .' Now I've gone Anglo-Indian.

Re-enter **Fraser**.

How do Americans say 'red'?

Fraser   Commie bastard.

Ilse   No! Red! Red!

Fraser *(to* **Pat***)*   You're the expert.

Pat *tries hard and gets a reasonable American.*

Pat   When the red, red, robin comes bob, bob, bobbing along, along . . .

Fraser   *Bang on!*

Ilse (*half convinced*)   It sounds OK, yes?

Fraser   *Mein schöner Engel!* He's brilliant! Talk to him . . .

They're both aware of **Fraser** *wanting to bring them together. Even* **Ilse** *is touched with a certain shyness.*

Ilse (to **Pat**)   You see, I learned English English. The first job I had was being a maid to a man and his wife in the control commission . . . Percival and Helen Trentham, both professors from Oxford, so I think I want to speak like them. But when I met some Americans they laughed at my English accent. If I'm going to get a secretary job in the American sector I have to speak American . . .

Pat   No . . . you don't need to . . .

Ilse   Yes I do! They don't like the British. They told me.

Fraser   Well, we can take them or leave them, can't we, Pat?

Pat   Never met one.

Fraser   Then you're in the best position to hang on to your prejudices . . . Personally I prefer the French . . .

Ilse   Not the French!

Fraser   I have some very good friends in the French sector. I mean, how else would you get the occasional truffle or foie gras? This came from there, incidentally.

Fraser *has now poured each of them a glass of wine.*

Pat   I've never tasted wine before . . .

Fraser   Never?

Pat   Only beer . . .

Ilse   My God!

Pat *sips his wine, is doubtful for a moment, then slowly nods.*

Fraser   This calls for a toast! To Bacchus!

Pat   Bacchus?

Fraser   That statue over there in the roses . . . you see him? The little fellow with the grapes and his balls shot off.

Ilse   That's the Russians. They always did that.

Pat   What?

Fraser   Shot the balls off. They did it all over the city. Stalin gave the order, didn't he? Long live the revolution, forward with the people and, when you get to Berlin, shoot the balls off all the statues.

Pat   So there could have been Russians in this garden?

Fraser   Oh yes.

Ilse   To hell with it! All I want to do is get out and get far away! I shall get a job with the Americans, because you get a lot more money and some girls who work for them . . . I know this . . . they get free flights to New York.

Pat   How?

Ilse   They've got these big, big transport planes that bring things over and go back empty. They sneak you on there! You fly for nothing!

Pat   You'd go?

Ilse   Of course! From here? I'd go to New York tomorrow. Show me a plane and I'd go today! The Russians will never stop till they've taken Berlin and they're poorer than we are! So why shouldn't I want to get out? America is rich. They believe in the right thing. They believe in things in the pocket . . . we believe in things in the head! That's why we got nothing.

Fraser   *Süsslein!* I'm hurt! You always have me to turn to!

She laughs and embraces him. **Fraser** *gives* **Pat** *a look over her shoulder.*

And now you have Pat . . .

But **Pat** *is lost in thought.*

Pat   I saw a Russian the other day . . . I'd seen them from the train and on guard at the war memorial . . . but this one was really close up.

Ilse (*sarcastic*)   Oh, how wonderful for you!

Pat   When I got to Charlottenburg I was told the Russian zone was only half a mile away and that their wire ran through the wood . . . the Grunewald. I wanted to see it, so I took a walk in there and caught a glimpse of it through the trees . . . but I felt a bit conspicuous . . . not a soul about . . . me in uniform . . . So the next day I was in HQ Sergeants' Mess and I met Quartermaster Ross . . . (*To* **Fraser**.) D'you know him?

Fraser   Dickie Ross, yes! Mess president.

Pat   Yes. Well, he has a dog, a big Alsatian . . .

Fraser   Max . . .

Pat   Max. I offered to take him for a walk. I took him into the wood. I thought if I had a dog with me it would look more casual . . . and I could get nearer the wire.

Ilse   Why? It's just wire! Haven't you seen wire before?

Fraser   Did you get there?

Pat   At first I couldn't see anything anywhere . . . Just trees. Max is in heaven, snuffling about . . . running this way and that . . . then suddenly there it was, thirty yards away. Took me totally by surprise. Not only wire but a sentry box with a young Russian sentry . . . and I mean young. Younger than me! Looked seventeen. Blue eyes, blond hair . . . very light blond hair . . .

Fraser   Ah! Bless him . . .

Pat   I froze. Hadn't bargained for this but Max . . . he just saw him as another human being . . . didn't know he was supposed to be the enemy . . . goes bounding up to him, wagging his tail! The Russian has a tommy gun on his shoulder and, as Max ran up to him, he unslings it. I thought: Jesus, he's going to shoot him! I'll have to go back to the quartermaster and say: I'm sorry, your dog's been shot by a Russian. But all he was doing was just propping the gun against the fence so he could pat him and play with him. He pulled his ears and shouted something . . . I don't know . . . the usual thing, like: He's a big fellow . . . must eat a lot of meat. And I should have said something back. Didn't matter if he didn't understand. I didn't understand. But I should have. Yet . . . I couldn't speak. Stuck like a post in the ground. Not a word. I wanted to say something . . .

Ilse   Why?

Pat   Why not? What did it need? The sky to fall in before I'd speak?

Ilse   He was probably saying: Does your sister jig-jig . . . something typically Russian like that.

Fraser   She's not much time for Russians.

Ilse   Me? I am one.

Fraser (*sardonic*)   Oh yes . . .

Ilse   I'm a quarter Russian. My grandmother was from Odessa.

Pat   Really?

Ilse   They say she had beautiful dark red hair!

Fraser   Well, that proves it then.

Pat   D'you speak Russian?

Ilse   A little. D'you?

Pat   No.

Fraser   In that case she speaks it very well . . .

Pat   I learned one word . . . well, two words . . .

Ilse   What?

Pat   *Ya sdayoos.* (*Now embarrassed.*) Supposed to mean 'I surrender'. Does it? *Ya sdayoos?*

Ilse   Where d'you learn that?

Pat   Someone at Hanover station. Said I might need it in Berlin. Useful phrase.

Ilse *reverts to her nervy, angry manner.*

Ilse   Don't say that! Not to me. I was here! I've seen them here!

Fraser   I tell you what, children: let us blow away the blues. Let us disport ourselves . . . *uns belustigen*! Ilse, shall we initiate our sergeant into what we do on Fridays after school?

Ilse   He can't do that. He's on duty.

Fraser   Of course he can! Show what we get up to in Charlottenburg when the evening shadows fall . . . when we pleasure ourselves . . .

Ilse *joins in the tease.*

Ilse   He may not like it.

Fraser   Oh . . . he'll like it. And we can use the bed.

He indicates to **Ilse** *who helps him to move the bed, side on to the audience.* **Fraser** *undoes the mattress and rolls it out.*

We drink a little wine. We put ourselves in a receptive mood. We make ourselves comfortable . . .

He sits on the bed facing the audience. **Ilse** *sits alongside him and he gestures to* **Pat** *to sit on her other side.* **Pat** *does this very warily.*

And once we're relaxed. Once we're at ease . . .

Puts an arm round **Ilse** *and waits for* **Pat** *to do the same.*

We watch a movie. Now I bet that surprises you, Pat. You are saying: How can they watch a movie? The answer is that Uncle Fraser has brought it here specially.

Pat   Here? Now?

Fraser   I prefer to see it in civilised company, don't I, *Liebling*? Far away from the hairy-arsed, nose-picking common soldiery!

He gets up and makes for the door.

But first we have to settle the matter of the logbook. It's about time that I was entered as having left. So, what I suggest . . . it's your choice, Pat . . . I suggest that I go outside now . . . in reality to get the cans of film from my Volks . . . but that you recognise it, technically, as a departure and write it in accordingly. I have to be gone by evening anyway . . . It's only a slight discrepancy in time.

Pat *feels bravado is called for.*

Pat   OK.

Fraser   Good.

He exits to the hall.

Ilse   Will you really help me . . . with American?

Pat   If you want me to.

Ilse   I'm not a Berliner. I'm from a village called Grossau, near Stettin in Pomerania . . . in the East. If the Russians take the city people like me will be sent back . . .

Pat   Go the other way. Go to Hanover. Go to West Germany.

Ilse   And if they invade there . . . if they take all . . . all Germany . . .

Pat   They won't . . . They're not going to.

He says this with conviction. She mistakes it for defiance and laughs.

Ilse   With you to stop them, Sergeant! *Ya sdayoos!*

Kisses his cheek as **Fraser** *enters carrying film cans.*

Fraser   Ah! What's been gestating while I've been away? Remember, children, it was Uncle Fraser who brought you together. Now, officially, I've gone. Come on Pat. Stick it in the log.

Pat *goes to the logbook, glances at his watch for the time and makes the entry.*

Pat   Right. (*Writes.*) Staff Sergeant Cullen . . .

Fraser (*spelling*)   C-U-L-L-E-N.

Pat (*writes*)   Departed. (*To* **Fraser**.) When you went, did you take the projector?

Fraser *starts to load the first reel.*

Fraser   Yes, put that . . . since I'll be taking it later. As for Ilse, we could look upon this as a brief interlude on her way home, which she is in the process of travelling towards, in which case she's already left . . . or she's not here.

Ilse   Don't get him in trouble. Put me in. I'm going to give up the job anyway. OK, baby? I take the rap. That's the show business!

Pat *makes no entry for her. He closes the book.*

Pat   You don't need 'the'. It's not 'That's "the" show business' . . . just: 'That's show business.'

She's delighted.

Ilse   That's show business! (*To* **Fraser**.) My teacher!

Fraser   Isn't he nice? For a sergeant, I mean.

Ilse   Well, you see, I look at his face and in it is something from England we don't have here . . .

Pat   I think 'inexperience' is the word you could be looking for.

Ilse   No. I see green fields with streams and . . . those little houses with the *Strohdach* on the top . . .

Fraser   Thatch. She means cottages . . .

Ilse   Cottages! Yes!

Pat   She looks at my face and sees cottages?

Ilse   No . . . peace! That's what I mean . . . peace! I see peace there.

She hugs him as he sits beside her on the bed. **Fraser** *has the film in place and stands behind them to operate the projector, pointing out over the audience.*

Fraser   Now, children, take hands. We're about to journey down a smoking pathway of light to the world of dreams and reach that golden spot in paradise where all our yearnings will be sweetly satisfied . . . You'll have to imagine the ice-cream girls and the mighty Wurlitzer. Cuddle your lover for reel one!

Projector is on, light flickering. We follow the opening in sound, into the Twentieth Century Fox fanfare followed by the Gershwinesque opening music track of an American movie.

Fraser, *standing by the projector, smiles down at his 'charges', now hand in hand on the bed, looking over the audience at the screen, all expectation.*

Blackout.

Scene Five

Night, some hours later.

Pat *sits staring out into the garden, a glass of wine before him. One bottle of wine is now empty; the other is a quarter full. Behind him* **Ilse** *stands 'outside time' . . . a character in a story.*

The desk is roughly laid with knives and forks for two, a dish of potato salad and a pot of mustard. **Fraser** *has gone and so has the projector.*

The actor playing **Pat** *speaks to the audience:*

Pat   He said . . . by the time the film had ended so had the day. Fraser had left, taking his projector with him . . . pandering to the last . . . persuading Ilse to stay with Pat . . . yet leaving an awkwardness in the air now the lights were on and the caressing had stopped. Ilse wanted to eat. She'd found some bockwurst in the kitchen. She said:

Isle   I'm sorry there's no sauerkraut. I know how the English love sauerkraut.

Pat   Pat remembers desperately wanting to get back close to her. But her mood had changed. He said, 'As it happens, I do love sauerkraut.'

They are in real time. He tries to take her wrist but she avoids him and exits to the kitchen with:

Ilse   Well there isn't any.

Pat   Pat said he distracted his mind from her by trying to think of the two in the corner of the garden who would get no meal . . . Had they been his age? Were they calm or savage in death? How did they face up to the storm that once blew over these elegant suburbs when Marshal

Zhukov's tanks came screaming out of the woods like Judgement Day?

Ilse enters with a steaming pan and plates. She forks out hot bockwurst sausages.

She becomes aware of him staring at her.

Ilse   What's the matter?

Pat   Would you go to London?

Ilse   Would you like me to?

Pat   Yes.

Ilse   Do you live in London?

Pat   I could if you were there.

Ilse   Can you get me a free ticket?

Pat   Well . . .

Ilse   Can you get me on a plane?

Pat   I don't know . . .

Ilse   It has to be America. There's no money in Britain.

Pat   Christ, you go on about money!

Ilse   So I should. I bet you'll have it.

Pat   I doubt it.

Ilse   You will. What will you be?

Pat   Not sure. The idea was to be an architect.

Ilse   A what? Architect? Is that what you will do?

Her imagination is caught for a moment.

Pat   I see all these ruins and I think: what's the point?

Ilse returns more cynically to her theme.

Ilse   Oh yes! You'll have money.

Pat   If you wanted help to get to London . . .

Ilse   I can't go to London! Can't you see? The British won't let us on military planes . . . the Americans will! And it has to be a plane. Otherwise I must get out through a Russian checkpoint on the road through the zone and they send me back! Eat your bockwurst. Then you can teach me American.

Pat   Ilse, I've never talked to an American in my life.

Ilse   You know how they speak from the movies . . .

Pat   So do you . . .

Ilse   You don't want to. OK. I'll go. I'll go home.

Pat   No. Don't go.

Ilse   Why should I stay?

Pat   To look after me.

Ilse   I've done enough looking after you!

Pat   You can't leave me with those ghosts.

Ilse   Which ghosts?

Pat   Those two out there . . .

Ilse   They're all right. I don't fear of them. There were so many like them. Sometimes, at night, I think they come to the window . . .

Pat   You've seen them?

Ilse   No . . . but I know when they're there. They look in. They see us when we don't see them. They don't blame anyone. They don't come hurting anyone. They're just sad that they're dead and we live.

Pat   Why aren't they angry? They should be. They get shot for being our enemies and a year later they're our friends . . . and the friends who shot them are 'the enemy'. It's like a dance.

Ilse   I was your enemy once.

Her tone is challenging. **Pat** *doesn't know what to say. She indicates the food.*

Eat. It's getting cold.

They eat for a while.

Pat   I've never seen a corpse.

Ilse   Never? You . . . a soldier!

Pat   Actually I tell a lie. I did see my grandmother in her coffin . . .

Ilse (*suddenly wistful*)   You saw her? Your grandmother?

Pat   I was seven. I was lifted up to see.

Ilse   I never saw mine.

Pat   But you've seen the dead?

Ilse   Oh yes. And I saw my father.

She stops.

Pat   He's dead?

Ilse   We had a farm in Grossau. When we saw our army retreating we packed our things to get out the next morning . . . but at first light we hear a Russian tank drive into the farmyard. The noise they make! Have you ever heard tanks?

Pat   Yes . . .

Ilse   My mother opened my bedroom window and pushed me out on the roof . . . in the snow . . . and told me to go to Berlin to my aunt's house. I got to the middle of the field and I turned to look back. I saw them bring my father out of the front door and shoot him on the doorstep.

Pat   They shot him?

Ilse   Yes. In his head. He bent over very quickly . . . and dropped.

Pat   Why did they shoot him?

Ilse   *Weiss nicht. Weiss nicht.*

Pat   What about your mother?

Ilse   I didn't see Mother. I ran away! I just ran! Then I did as I was told . . . I walked to Berlin . . . two hundred kilometres! My aunt's house had gone . . . nothing! You couldn't even see the street. The fighting came in the city and I had to hide. I looked in a cellar and at the bottom of the steps there were these soldiers in a heap where they'd been killed. German soldiers. Seven of them. They looked terrible . . . dreadful! But I had to go past them to hide. I was more afraid of what was outside than I was of them.

Pat   What was outside?

Ilse   Cossacks and Tartars getting drunk, riding up and down on horses, shooting at street lamps. It was a good place to hide, that cellar. Anyone who opened the door saw the corpses and went away.

Pat   Didn't they smell?

Ilse   No more than me. Any water you got was to drink, not to wash.

Pat   How long did you have to stay there?

Ilse   I don't know. Weeks. What were you doing when you were sixteen?

Pat   I was at school . . .

Ilse   Well, that was my school. Two other girls joined me and we crept out at night to find something to eat. You know what we ate?

Pat   What?

Ilse   This is not very nice for your friend Max . . . We ate dogs. You've heard of this? There were dead dogs all over the city . . . not cats. The cats crawl away when the bombs fall but the dogs run around and get killed. Except the ones who are chained up. And they get killed because they're chained up.

Pat   You ate one?

Ilse   Oh, we ate more than one! You know, in the bad times after the first war, in the 1920s, people ate dogs then. So we know all about eating dogs. I remember the first one. We could see its tail, pointing up out of the bricks. He was a . . . *Wachtelhund* (*searches for the English word*) spaniel . . . brown and white. We cut off his hair with a bread knife and ate him in pieces.

Pat   Raw?

Ilse   What? (*Realises.*) No! No! We cooked him with some salt! What d'you think we were . . . barbarians?? They say a dog is your best friend. It's true!

Pat *hears something in the garden.*

Pat   What's that? That slithering sound . . .

She goes to the garden doors, still chewing bread.

Ilse   Oh, it must be the wind. There's a cloth . . . what d'you say? . . . 'oil cloth', hanging in the broken glass house. It swishes about.

Pat   I hadn't noticed any wind.

Ilse   You can feel it over here . . .

He goes to her.

Feel it on your face.

She touches his face, lightly.

You've gone sad. It's all this talk of death.

Pat   It's the wine . . .

Ilse   Eat some of my sausage. Talk of something else.

She breaks off a piece of sausage. They stand, eating and wondering what next. Then:

You know there's a dance tomorrow night?

Pat   No . . .

Ilse   Oh, Pat! At the British Services Club at Reichskanzlerplatz.

Pat   Oh yes . . .

Ilse   It's a charity ball . . . a big event. Even the Americans come to it.

Pat   So you want to go . . .

Ilse   Oh no . . . I can't go.

Pat   If I took you . . . ?

Ilse   You certainly can't go! You have to be here.

Pat   Then why mention it?

Pat *thinks he's being played with.*

Ilse   I wondered if you knew . . .

Pat   Strange thing to wonder if you can't go!

Ilse   You weren't like this when we watched the movie.

Pat   Yes, well . . . that's over.

A moment of stillness then he takes the plate from her and kisses the palm of her hand.

Suddenly they embrace hard, almost falling. They steady one another. She searches his face. He can't stand the scrutiny and turns his face away.

Ilse   Show me your face. Show me! I like to see your face . . .

Pat   Are you looking for cottages?

Ilse   I'm looking for you.

He kisses her again, then leads her to the bed.

Not the bed! The 'mortuary' bed. It's not good here. I work
here. This is my office . . .

Pat *flares up again, thinking she's rejecting him.*

Pat   If you're going to go, go now! Go quickly!

Ilse   I didn't say I was going to go.

She kisses him. Calms him.

When I stay late . . . work late there's something I
sometimes do if I'm alone . . . I go upstairs and have a bath.
There's a big old bathroom up there with a great long tub
that you can almost swim in. Much better than where I live,
which only has a shower. There's a gas boiler which is very
slow but very hot. But the light's broken . . . which doesn't
matter so much because we have plenty of candles . . .

*She takes candles from a drawer. He stands uncertainly, still resentful.
From another drawer she takes out a folded bath towel.*

And there's a towel the size of an elephant from the old, old
days. I found it lost at the back of a drawer and keep it just
for me. I think it's from the Kaiser's time. It's very imperial,
don't you think? Feel it. Room to expand . . . I've gone mad
now . . . so you must go mad. Both be mad, OK? You wait
down here while I make it ready. I fill it . . . put candles
round it. It's something I really love. You should see when
the candles are lit and the water makes lights in the room
. . . little waving lights. And sometimes the moon shines on
the window which has blue and pink squares of glass. Wait.
Give me a few minutes. I'll call you. (*Blows a kiss.*) *Ya sdayoos!*

She moves to the door.

And you can bring some more candles.

She exits. **Pat** *is transfixed. The wind blows in the garden, rain falls.
He's a little daunted at first by the thought of* **Ilse** *and the bath. Then
he goes to the desk and takes out more candles. One of them he sticks
into the neck of a wine bottle and lights it. He turns off the room lights*

and enjoys the effect of the flame. By the light of the candle he takes off his boots and gaiters, now and then listening for sounds upstairs.

Suddenly there is a tapping at the garden window. We hear a man's voice, low spoken:

Voice   *Entschuldigen! . . . Wächter! . . .* Wächter Stahl . . . Can you give me help, please?

Pat *is panicked as though the ghosts he'd been talking about had actually materialised.*

 Pat   Who is it?

The door seems to blow open and a powerfully built man enters. He looks, at a glance, like a German soldier, wearing a rain-wet oilskin coat over a grey uniform and a Wehrmacht style forage cap. In one hand he carries a pick handle, the other hand being roughly bound in a bloodstained rag.

Dieter   Dieter Stahl, Sergeant . . . watchman. Did Captain Wirral say about me? The nightwatchman . . .

Dieter *fishes out an identity card and shows it.*

Pat (*realising*)   Watchman! Yes. He mentioned something.

Dieter (*indicating candle*)   You have problem with the electric?

Pat *hastily switches on the lights.*

Pat   No, no. I was going to read by it . . . in bed. (*Indicates the bed.*) You don't have to get out to the light switch.

Dieter   Ah, *ja* . . . understand . . .

We get the feeling he doesn't really believe this.

Pat   You cut your hand?

Dieter   A little. I'm stupid. On the wire.

Pat   Wire?

Dieter *Ja* . . . it's on top of the gate. I know it's there but still I get my hand on it. Stupid! There's a box in the kitchen.

Pat First aid? I'll get it . . .

Dieter No, you stay here, Sergeant. I know where.

He exits. **Pat** *doesn't want him wandering around the house and stays in the doorway waiting for him to return. He hopes* **Ilse** *has heard and will stay quiet and that the faint sound of running water won't be heard.*

Dieter *returns pressing a piece of sticking plaster over cotton wool on the base of his thumb.*

Pat Done?

Dieter OK. I have plenty of holes in me already. I was also a sergeant . . . I was for two years by the Russian front.

Pat *nods but can't help glancing upwards.* **Dieter** *looks up with him.* **Pat** *has to explain.*

Pat It's the bath running. I started it just now.

Dieter Ah . . . nice hot bath. I will go. Thank you, Sergeant.

Pat D'you come again before morning?

Dieter Not unless you want. You are here, *ja*? I don't come till Monday.

Pat No . . . that's fine.

Dieter But you will enter in your book that I was here at this time . . . OK?

Pat Of course.

Dieter So. I leave you to your bath . . . and your wine . . .

Pat Oh . . . have a glass . . .

Dieter No, no . . .

Pat   Please! There's plenty.

Pat *wipes* **Fraser**'s *glass and pours. They toast.*

Dieter   *Prosit!*

Pat   *Prosit!*

Dieter *notices* **Pat**'s *book.*

Dieter   Your bed book . . .

Pat   Yes . . .

Dieter   Turgenev . . .

Pat   You know him?

Dieter   Yeah, I know Turgenev. (*A moment, then:*) He's dead.

Pat *can't be sure how this is meant.*

Pat   Yes, he's dead.

Dieter   Oh yes. (*He enjoys the bitterness of the joke.*) You hear of the big panzer battle at Prokhorovka near Kursk in '43? That's where he died . . . Turgenev, in a burning tank. He got himself out . . . smoke coming from him . . . he crawled in the grass pulling himself along, so much did he want to live. I get him. I lay him by a wall . . . give him a cigarette . . . but in two minutes he's gone. I saw them all. They all went . . . all of them, between here and Stalingrad. Who d'you want . . . Dostoevsky? Cut in half by twenty-millimetre bullets at Novgorod. Ask me! Anyone! Mozart? Straight through the head at Lutsk. Beethoven? Drowns in the Pripet River when his truck turned over . . . and I couldn't reach him! I try! *Scheisse!* I try! But I couldn't reach! I'm this far from him! (*Then:*) Here's to them.

He raises his glass. **Pat** *does the same.*

Pat   Here's to them . . .

Dieter   *Tot . . . fertig . . . vorüber.* All Europe is now in the earth. They've all gone and it's all gone with them, my

friend. That world is over. We kill it. Now come the
Amerikaners. *Macht nichts.* OK. *C'est la vie. À votre santé.*
(*Drains glass.*) *Spazeba*! Thank you, Sergeant. Good sleep!
Good night!

Pat   Good night.

Dieter *exits to the garden.* **Pat** *is greatly troubled by the encounter.*
Enter **Ilse** *half dressed with clothes bundled up. She puts out the light
so that only the candle is burning.*

Ilse   Did he know I was here?

Pat   No. I told him I was running the water.

Ilse   He knew.

Pat   He said . . .

Ilse   I know what he said. What he always says.

She dresses quickly.

Why did he come in?

Pat   He'd cut his hand. He wanted the first-aid box.

Ilse   I don't believe it. He'll go down to the military police
post and then come back. If I'm quick I can get to the
station before he does. Then when he comes back ask him
in again and let him see there's no one else here! If you
don't you'll be in trouble. Oh God, I'm breaking my shoe!

She grabs her things.

Pat   What about tomorrow?

Ilse   I can't! I'm sorry. We're not lucky, are we? If you
look up there you'll see it's like I told you. The moon's
shining through the window . . . like I said . . .

She reaches out to **Pat**. *He doesn't respond.*

Fade to black.

Act Two

Scene One

The same, late morning the next day. Hot, brilliant day; lazy summer sounds. The stage is deserted. The bed has evidently been slept in, blankets and sheets are tumbled about; **Pat**'s *boots and webbing thrown on the floor. The front door bell rings a time or two.* **Pat** *appears from the garden, sleepily. He's nodded off sitting reading in the sun. He is barefoot and wears only his army issue green underpants. He pulls on his khaki shirt, rapidly buttoning it up as he comes in. On his head he wears an old, battered straw gardening hat he's found. He looks round vaguely for his trousers. As he does so,* **Fraser** *enters from the garden carrying a small zip-up bag.*

Fraser Oh Schoolie, Schoolie, Schoolie! Hadn't we the strength left to crawl to the door? What did she do to you?

Pat I was in the garden . . .

Fraser You were asleep!

Pat I was reading . . .

Fraser Oh, there's no sleep like the sleep of a satisfied lover. It's called satiation. You're educated. You know that word: 'satiation'! There is no finer word in the dictionary! If I was shipwrecked on a desert island and I could only take one word with me, Schoolie, that word would be satiation. And if I could take one more word it would be 'utter' . . . utter satiation. How many times, eh? I bet you didn't close your eyes till dawn. Did she bring you to your knees? Did she smoke it, Schoolie? That's what the world wants to know
. . . Did she smoke it?

Pat Maybe I did drop off. I had this dream . . .

He recalls a dream that was far from pleasant.

Fraser What dream?

Pat (*evasive*)   Oh, the sort where you float in mid-air . . . looking down from high up . . .

Fraser   Flying! You don't need much interpretation there! All flying dreams are sexual, aren't they? It's well known. No . . . I've read about this . . . the sexual urge is nothing more or less than the suppressed human desire to grow feathers and fly. The theory is that we were all birds in a previous existence and sex is the memory of it. Next time you've nothing better to do take a look at the underside of your scrotum and see if it doesn't resemble the skin of a plucked, flightless bird. You can see the marks where the quills of the feathers once were . . . like a Christmas turkey.

He notes **Pat** *searching around.*

You lost something?

Pat   My trousers.

Fraser   Oh well, then, that's love, isn't it? That's the real thing! Losing your heart . . . you could fake that. But not losing your trousers!

Pat (*looks under bed*)   I left them on the floor . . .

Fraser   Look at that bed. Rejected, cast-off and despised . . . But last night was its finest hour . . . and I bet it's seen some action in its time. The German Wehrmacht is proud to have placed that bed at your disposal. How was she, Schoolie? Tell me all about it.

Pat *wonders if he knows already.*

Pat   Ask her. She's next door . . .

Fraser   No she's not.

Pat   How do you know?

Fraser   She phoned me this morning.

Pat *tries not to give away his desperation to talk to* **Ilse**.

Pat   Would you give me her number?

Fraser   Can't . . .

Pat   What's her number? I want to speak to her!

Fraser   She doesn't have a phone. She has to do the ringing.

Pat   How is she?

Fraser   Like a woman who knows she's been loved, Pat. She said, I love my sergeant . . . he soothes me . . . *beruhigt mich!*

Pat   You're making it up.

Fraser   No! Me? I could practically hear her smiling at the other end! You know what she said about last night?

Pat (*wary*)   What?

Fraser   'Heavenly.' That was her word. 'Heavenly.' I do think a touch of religion improves a good fuck, don't you?

Pat *almost responds angrily.*

Fraser   Your trousers are in the garden. Back of the iron seat.

Pat *exits to the garden to get them.* **Fraser** *now shows some concern. After a moment he takes three bottles of Mâcon from the bag and puts them on the desk. He collects up the three empty bottles and puts them in the bag.* **Pat** *returns with the trousers.*

I only came for the empties. Listen . . . I've got a friend of yours outside in the Volks. I said I'd see what state you were in.

Pat   Who?

Fraser   If only you'd told me you'd met him. He's an old mucker of mine . . . always in and out of Berlin.

Pat   Who?

Fraser   You played tennis with him in Hanover.

He says this as he exits to the front door. **Pat** *is annoyed and disturbed by the news. He scrambles to do up his trousers and clip his belt in place, finds his socks and is still putting them on when* **Clive** *enters followed by* **Fraser.**

Clive And once again we're ships that pass at noon, Sergeant. You remember that? . . . Twelve o'clock, the hour of no shadows? The red dust?

Pat So there was red dust!

Clive Did I say there wasn't?

Pat Yes.

Clive (*to* **Fraser**) He'll pick an argument over anything, this one! I was describing you to Fraser in the car . . . I said I'd met this Ed sergeant who's an interesting combination of the easy-going and the argumentative. He said: I know who that is.

Fraser He's talking bull.

Clive (*to* **Fraser**) Well, introduce me . . .

Fraser (*to* **Pat**) Of course. Staff Sergeant Clive Burns . . . Sergeant Pat Harford.

They shake hands.

Pat I thought you were an officer, Staff . . .

Clive I know you did. (*Glances down at* **Pat**'s *feet.*) Don't let me stop you putting your boots on.

Though this is said lightly, **Pat** *takes it as an admonishment. He counters, innocently, glancing down at* **Clive**'s *feet.* **Clive** *is wearing shoes (associated with being off duty).*

Pat I was going to wear shoes . . .

Clive Why not? We're not on parade, are we? And, as you say, I don't hold His Majesty's commission so who am I to get regimental?

Fraser *is fascinated by the tension* **Pat** *feels in* **Clive**'s *presence.* **Pat** *puts on the shoes.*

Fraser   Clive likes to be a man of mystery, you see . . . and, it has to be said, he has a lot to be mysterious about.

Clive *has moved to the garden doors. He looks out.*

Clive   Is that the burial ground?

Fraser   That's the one. (*To* **Pat**.) I'll stick these in the kitchen.

He takes the three bottles of wine and exits to the hall.

Clive   Did you see your Russians from the train?

Pat   Hundreds.

Clive   Doing what?

Pat   Going for a pee. Going to the cook house.

Clive   What did you make of them?

Pat   Well, they walk about and talk and breathe just like us, really.

Clive   Not breathe. They don't breathe like us. They don't breathe like us at all. We breathe air. They have to breathe this red dust you were talking about. Don't they? (*Then:*) Fraser says you read Russian literature . . .

Fraser *returns.*

Fraser   What was that?

Clive *ignores him.*

Clive (*to* **Pat**)   Do you?

Pat   Yes I do.

Fraser   Do what?

Clive (*to* **Fraser**)   Hang on! (*To* **Pat**.) Why?

Pat   What d'you mean why?

Clive   Why do you read the Russians?

Fraser *is now guilty that he passed this on.*

Fraser   Oh that . . .

Clive (*persisting*)   Why do you?

Pat   I expect, to be honest, it's because I've been told that I should. That they're works of genius. But when I read them I just enjoy what I read.

Clive (*cutting across*)   Ever read Tolstoy? . . . *War and Peace*?

Pat   No . . . I shall, though. There's a case in point . . . People say read it because it's the world's greatest novel . . .

Clive   Bollocks.

Pat   My father thinks so.

Clive   Does he? Bollocks. I haven't read it all but I have most of it. Certainly the biggest. But, I mean, it doesn't touch Shakespeare.

Pat   It's a novel . . .

Clive   It doesn't touch Shakespeare! Come on! It can't, can it?

Pat   If you say so . . .

Clive   But . . . but . . . I'm saying read it. And there's a reason to do so. Every thinking Russian has read *War and Peace* . . . so reading it helps get you into the mind of the thinking Russian and it's the thinking Russian we're up against.

Fraser   That's a relief. If we're only up against thinking Russians we'll have a walkover.

Clive   So what's your considered assessment of the situation, Fraser?

Fraser   Call me a silly old cinema manager but I thought we were surrounded and outnumbered twenty to one.

Clive   So what do we do?

Fraser   Eat, drink and shag ourselves stupid.

Clive   I don't know, Fraser . . . I don't know. What do a couple of battle-scarred veterans, who once shook the desert sand from their socks . . . who've gone through shit and shellfire from Alamein to the Elbe; who stood on the brink of taking Berlin but were wrongfully held back so the fucking Reds could take it . . . what wisdom in a so-called peaceful post-war world can we impart to our young friend here? He's got to teach classes for the next eighteen months . . . so what's he going to teach 'em, these outnumbered squaddies, ringed around by the Russian hordes? Those lads need something positive to cling to, don't they? They don't want to be told that the enemy is a 'genius' or 'the greatest'. They need to have reinforced their pride in their own . . . and even if they wouldn't know Shakespeare if he pissed in their mess tins, they want to know that the invincible spirit we had at Agincourt is not, repeat not, going to desert us now. Teaching's like anything else; you can teach positively or you can teach negatively . . . assuming you know the difference.

Pat   Well, yes . . . I think I do, yes . . .

Clive   You do?

Pat   I know I do.

Clive   What is it?

Pat   If I tell them that the world's greatest playwright is English, that's positive. If I tell 'em the greatest novelist is Russian . . . that's negative.

Fraser (*to* **Clive**)   What d'you think?

Clive *smiles easily and glances at his watch.*

Clive   I've got to move.

Fraser   Right with you. Just a quick word with Pat.

Clive   No, I'll walk. God knows I need the exercise.

Fraser   Two tics, that's all . . .

Clive   I'm walking. See you there. (*Then to* **Pat**.) Nice shot, Sergeant . . . Fifteen love.

Pat   Thanks, Staff.

Exit **Clive**.

Fraser   Why's he walking? What's he up to? He never walks.

Pat   He gets up my nose just like he did before.

Fraser   Well, he talks such a load of bull.

Pat   What's his name again?

Fraser   Clive. We used to call him 'Izzy' . . . whenever he left a room someone would always say 'Izzy gone?'

Pat   What's he do?

Fraser   You didn't notice?

Pat   No . . .

Fraser   He's a spook. Army intelligence.

Pat   How would I have known that?

Fraser   His badge . . .

Pat   They have a badge?

Fraser   His cap badge!

Pat   I didn't see it.

Fraser   Well, it was there!

Pat   You mean, if you're in secret intelligence you wear a badge telling everyone you're in secret intelligence? It's mad!

Fraser   Course it's mad . . . it's the army. (*Then:*) His mob have got a house near the Kaiserdamm. I was giving him a lift there.

He takes an envelope from his pocket.

Anyway, I've brought you a present. Two tickets for the dance tonight. So you can take Ilse.

Pat *is thrown.*

Fraser   Come on! Reichskanzlerplatz. The charity ball.

Pat   She said she couldn't go.

Fraser   Well, if she did she's changed her mind. She phoned me. She said you'd talked about it.

Pat   Why isn't she going with you?

Fraser   Me?

Pat   She gets on with you better than me . . .

Fraser   Oh Schoolie! I'm not a cradle-snatcher! You've been thinking there was something between her and me?

Pat   Isn't there?

Fraser   No, no, no! I should have said. I'm already spoken for!

Pat   Oh . . .

Fraser   Yes . . . oh! And she sulks just like you do . . . You'd get on well. This is my lovely lady . . .

He gets his wallet out and shows photo.

Gisela . . . you must meet her. Lives up at Tegel in the French sector. Trouble is we've got a party we can't get out of so we can't come. Otherwise I'd have taken her. (*Then:*) So . . . it's up to you.

Pat   I'm supposed to be on duty . . .

Fraser   With a break for dinner. That's two hours . . . stretch it to three . . . Three and a half? Take her for that long and bring her back here! Who'd know? Come on! It's destiny! There's a warm night forecast . . . and there's even a nightingale! It sings in a tree in a garden off Bismarckstrasse. Walk her that way back and you'll hear it in full song.

Pat   Will she phone me?

Fraser   It's all arranged. She'll be at the door at eight thirty.

Pat's confusion and vague suspicions boil over.

Pat   Something's going on! Ever since I got here you've never stopped pushing us together. What's it all about? She doesn't want me. If she did she'd ring me, not do it through you!

Fraser   Oh, are we going to have drama? I've no time for drama.

Pat   I don't know what to say to her. What have I seen? Nothing! Look what she's been through!

Fraser   Now you musn't believe everything she tells you.

Pat   They shot her father!

Fraser   Did they?

Pat   She said they shot him . . .

Fraser   Well, there you are.

Pat   Are you saying it isn't true?

Fraser   No, I'm not saying that.

Pat   When she got to Berlin. When she hid in the cellar . . .

He stops.

Fraser   Well?

Pat   Was she raped?

Fraser   I've never asked her.

Pat   Did the Russians rape her?

Fraser   I don't know! What d'you think? Come on, Schoolie! The world moves on. These are the things of long ago. Let 'em moulder! This dance is here and now!

He gets back in control.

Take her. She'll phone me. Do I tell her yes?

Pat   Why can't she phone me here?

Fraser   Is it yes?

Pat *knows he's going to give way.*

Pat   Yes.

Fraser   Got money?

Pat   For the tickets?

Fraser *declines being paid.*

Fraser   No, no, no . . . for drinks . . . for a flower.

Pat   What?

Fraser   You see, in the end, all she wants is romance, Schoolie. Simple old-fashioned romance. This was once a city of romance . . . strange as it may seem. Buy her a flower. One she can pin on her dress. Take a pin . . .

He gets a pin from the desk and hands it to him.

Stick it in your shirt. Then you've got it with you. There's a flower stall at Reichskanzlerplatz.

Pat   Eight?

Fraser   Eight thirty. She'll be there.

He exits. **Pat** *sticks the pin in his shirt.*

As he thinks troubled thoughts about the evening ahead, we hear the music of a thirty-piece showband, not in the mellow Glenn Miller mode, but the blaring harsh destructive discords of Stan Kenton's 'Peanut Vendor' echoing through the space of a vast dance hall.

Fade to black.

Scene Two

Later, after midnight. The room is now empty and in darkness; moonlight streams from the garden.

Sound of the front door being unlocked. A light is switched on in the hall. We see **Pat** *enter, back from the dance, wearing 'walking-out dress' i.e. shoes, battledress top, shirt and tie . . . loosened off on this hot night. He carries a paper bag with some food. Pausing in the doorway he speaks quietly to the unseen person in the hall.*

Pat   Hold on a minute . . . I'll take a look in the garden.

He moves through the darkened room to the garden doors and peers out. Satisfied, he turns on the lights.

OK, Lloyd . . . Come through . . .

US Army Corporal **Lloyd Jackson** *enters, his tunic unbuttoned, tie untied, carrying two bottles of beer. He takes in the room.*

Lloyd   Dear God! You were right. It's a palace!

Pat   I said there was plenty of room.

Lloyd (*indicating garden*)   Who did you think was out there?

Pat   No one . . .

Lloyd   The watchman?

Pat   No, I said . . . he won't be here till Monday. I was just checking.

Lloyd   The dead?

Pat   Oh, they're there.

Lloyd　There are worse places to end it.

Pat　Not when it was the last day of the war.

Lloyd　Was it?

Pat　Couldn't have been far off.

Lloyd *steps out into the garden.* **Pat** *quickly tidies some things away.* **Lloyd** *returns. He carefully observes* **Pat***.*

Lloyd　So. It's still OK?

Pat　Course it's OK.

Lloyd　Just asking.

Pat　You're the guest of the British Army, Lloyd.

Lloyd　I don't want to bring you no trouble.

There's an edge of bravado about **Pat***'s reply.*

Pat　No one's going to know. Anyway, you're stranded, you've missed your last transport, for Chrissake! We're supposed to be allies. What's that mean if it isn't helping one another?

Lloyd　I stay?

Pat　You stay.

Lloyd　Have a beer.

He hands **Pat** *one of the bottles.*

Got a church key?

Pat　What's a church key?

Lloyd　It opens bottles.

Pat　Oh . . . should be something in the kitchen . . . (*Suddenly puts on a posh accent, quoting 'Lives of a Bengal Lancer'*) Here are your orders . . .

Lloyd *joins in, very British.*

Pat/Lloyd　And this time, obey them!

Pat *exits.* **Lloyd** *moves around the room, observing it keenly. He ends up at the noticeboard as* **Pat** *returns with an opener.*

Lloyd   You know, this is the kind of place that the word 'bourgeois' was invented for. Would you want to live in it?

Pat   No. Well, that's ludicrous, saying no. If someone offered it, yes. Or if it was a house like this but not this one. I mean . . . it's begun to oppress me.

Lloyd   Because it's bourgeois?

Pat *is caught on the wrong foot by the thrust of the choice.*

Pat   Maybe. But more to do with what's happened in it and around it. Its past. Somebody lived here once.

Lloyd   Yeah. Someone generally did. It's what houses are for.

Pat *is surprised by* **Lloyd***'s sharpness of tone.*

Pat   I just wonder who they were.

Lloyd   You know who they were . . . The British took the house from the Nazis in '45. Who d'you think the Nazis took it from?

Pat   You think they were Jewish?

Lloyd   Sure they were Jewish . . .

Pat   They'd have to be.

Lloyd   The truck'd be in the driveway with its motor running. They'd be allowed one coat, one suitcase each. Everything else they'd leave.

Pat   That's what began to disturb me first . . . you could sense that it had been looted.

Lloyd   You bet it was looted. And let's say this Jewish family man and his wife were persons of culture . . . collectors. So there's a French Impressionist original hanging right up there.

Indicates a spot on the wall.

What d'you think? A Degas? A lesser known Manet? The Nazis sell the painting to the Swiss, who are famous for not asking questions . . . then . . . and here's the interesting bit . . . who d'you think the Swiss sell it to? New York.

Pat   After the war?

Lloyd   During the war, my friend. During the war! I know this for a fact: even while GIs were dying at Bastogne, New York dealers were secretly trading in paintings looted by the Nazis.

He thinks he hears someone.

Someone out front?

He takes look out in the hall and returns.

Pat   No?

Lloyd   No. Thought maybe it was your girl.

Pat   Ilse? . . . She's not 'my girl'.

Lloyd   Will she show up?

Pat   Not now. Well, she didn't, did she?

Lloyd   Could still.

Pat   You're trying to make me feel better. All right . . . I was stood up.

Lloyd   You don't seem too worried.

Pat   Why should I be? I got some good conversation out of it. She'll be sorry she didn't meet you. She wants to know all about America.

Lloyd   Is this where you watched the movie with her?

Pat   Right here. Screen that way.

Lloyd   You ever seen *The Grapes of Wrath*?

Pat   No . . .

Lloyd   See it. Tell her to see it. Henry Fonda. It's about union-busting in the Californian vineyards. That'll tell her about America.

*Pat notes **Lloyd**'s contemptuous tone.*

Pat   I'm not sure that's what she'd want to know. Cheers . . .

Lloyd   Cheers, my friend.

Pat   What about Britain . . .

Lloyd   What about Britain?

*He looks expectantly at **Pat** who now decides not to speak. A silence. Then **Lloyd** lightens the mood:*

Hey . . . I love the names of your regiments: the Green Howards . . . the Royal Inniskilling Fusiliers! And look what we've got here . . .

He points at a notice on the board.

'The Black Watch'! And, my God, this one: 'The Eleventh Hussars'!

Pat   Light tanks. There were a couple of their officers at the dance, wearing their evening blues . . . did you notice? They got little bits of chain mail on their shoulders . . .

Lloyd   Yeah, I saw those two. Like *Lives of a Bengal Lancer* . . .

Pat (*pukka accent*)   Steady on there, old chap. Hussars . . . not Lancers.

Lloyd (*follows suit*)   Awfully sorry, old boy. Is there a difference?

Pat   Hussars have sabres. Lancers have those long pointed thingies . . .

Lloyd   Do they? Dashed uncomfortable in the saddle . . .

Pat (*changing tone*)   Fuck 'em!

Lloyd   You don't like these people?

Pat   It's OK for you. Your army's democratic . . . We
have to take an oath of loyalty to the King . . . did you know
that? Hand on the Bible, right hand raised . . .

Lloyd   Not to the constitution?

Pat   We don't have a constitution! I said to myself: if I'm
going to be shot at I don't see the point of taking an oath to
a millionaire at the end of the Mall! (*Then:*) Have some
chicken.

They eat.

Lloyd   So what about the oath? You had to take it?

Pat   I went round the corner afterwards and untook it.
There's a word for that . . .

Lloyd   'Revoked'?

Pat   That'll do, yes . . . revoked it. Then I took another
oath . . . a personal oath . . . to my family, my friends . . . to
the local pub . . . to Parliament . . . to the people!

Lloyd   The people! My God! This they must never know!

Pat   I wondered . . . if you actually refused the oath . . .
refused it point blank . . . what would they do? Give you up?
Send you home?

Lloyd   D'you want to go home?

Pat   No.

Lloyd   No?

Pat   I only just got here. It's too interesting. I mean,
politically.

Lloyd   Are you political?

Pat   My father doesn't think I am, or, at least, not enough.
He says I never see the true political advantage. When I
complained about the call-up, about being conscripted, he

said: 'Don't say a word against national service. It's teaching a whole generation of socialists how to shoot.'

Lloyd   Is he a socialist?

Pat (*evasive*)   He's been a lot of things . . .

Lloyd   What about you?

Pat   Well . . . I mean . . . what is socialism?

Lloyd   The overthrow of the capitalist system and the gaining of social justice through collective means.

Pat *is thrown by the smoothness of the reply.*

Pat   Oh. Well, I don't think I'm ready to label myself yet.

Lloyd   Sure. But in the end you gotta go where your sympathies lie.

Pat *is disturbed by this. A silence.*

Pat   What's going to happen, Lloyd? What d'you think's going to happen? Are we going to wake up one morning soon and find the Russians have moved in?

Lloyd   They won't.

Pat   Why not?

Lloyd   We got the bomb, my friend.

Pat   So have they now.

Lloyd   Right. Nobody move!

Pat   That's it! No one moves. Are we all slowly disappearing into some kind of glacier? Will they come in a million years and dig out all these frozen armies like those hairy mammoths that they found under the ice? Is no one trying any more to find a way through?

Lloyd   Have you been east?

Pat   East Berlin?

Lloyd   East Berlin.

Pat   No . . . but I shall. Have you?

Lloyd   A couple of times.

Pat   What's it like?

Lloyd (*he hesitates*)   Well, it ain't Coney Island.

Pat   The standard British line on it is: 'You have an absolute legal right to go into the Soviet sector whenever you please. We just don't want you to.'

Lloyd   But you still want to go?

Pat   I shall go. No question.

Lloyd   Maybe we could go in together . . .

Pat   Why not? And we'll walk up to the first Russian soldiers we see and talk to them!

Lloyd   Before or after they arrest us?

Pat   There should be a thousand of us going over there every day! If enough of us went over just to talk . . . They can't arrest you for that.

Lloyd   Can't they? You make me think of the Russian joke about the two guys in the labour camp. One says: They put me in here for ten years and I'm completely innocent. The other says: Liar! If you're innocent you get twenty years!

Pat *likes the story and is curious about it.*

Pat   That's a real Russian joke?

Lloyd   Oh, they have them. Got it from a guy who's in the allied military mission at Potsdam.

Pat (*impressed*)   Really?

Pat *expects him to elaborate on this but he doesn't.*

Lloyd   Hey . . . I need the john . . .

Pat (*indicating the hall*)   Door on the left in the hall.

Lloyd   Then I guess it's bedtime.

He exits to the hall. **Pat** *ponders* **Lloyd***'s last remark. He stares at the bed, indecisively. Then, working quickly, he takes the blankets and sheets off the bed and pulls the mattress on to the floor.*

He walks round the bed, thinking. He lays out one blanket on the wire of the bedstead and the other on the mattress, together with the pillow. Finds a couple of cushions from the chairs and arranges them as pillows on the bed.

We hear the lavatory flush. **Pat** *sits and pretends to read but immediately dashes about putting one of the sheets on the mattress and one on the bedstead. Now he sits once more.*

Lloyd *re-enters and notes the change.*

Lloyd   So. Single beds?

Pat   It's a bit small . . . and it's the only one in the house.

Lloyd *'measures' the bed.*

Lloyd   Not so small.

Pat   Believe me . . . I thresh about a lot in my sleep.

Lloyd   How d'you know?

Pat   I've been told. As guest you get the mattress.

Lloyd   I can't have that. It's yours.

Pat   No . . . yours. The bed's OK for me like that. I've done this before.

Lloyd   Oh?

Pat *has guessed what's coming. He ducks out.*

Pat   Help yourself.

He exits to hall. **Lloyd** *thinks a moment, then gets out of his clothes, folding the pants and putting them with his tunic over a chair. Stripped to his underpants he fishes a notebook out of his tunic and scribbles notes in it. He checks the noticeboard. Hears flush of loo.* **Pat** *returns.*

Lloyd   Just doing my diary. You do one?

Pat   Never got past January the fifth.

Lloyd *indicates the noticeboard.*

Lloyd   I always thought it was two 'z's in Hussar . . .

Pat   Two 's's.

Lloyd   Yeh. Two 'z's is the cheer . . .

Pat   Huzzah!

Lloyd   Huzzah!

Pat *begins to undress.* **Lloyd** *carries on making notes.*

Pat   What will it say? The diary.

Lloyd   About tonight?

Pat   Yes.

Lloyd   I don't know. It's not over yet. I may say: I met this British guy at the dance at Reichskanzlerplatz . . . how we got away from the noise and had a few beers and we talked and put the world to rights . . . But I will probably say I worry about him.

Pat   Why?

Lloyd   I'll say that it's just our luck to be young when the earth's been left a smoking ruin . . . though we could have had worse luck if we'd been born earlier and gone through the fire ourselves. There was a guy after the war who said, when people look back on this century, they'll call it the century of destruction. It's what we're good at . . . destruction. So for you and me it's a matter of not being destroyed. In a time like this, Pat, the important thing is to survive. Not just in the flesh but in the spirit.

Pat   Are you religious?

Lloyd   No, but I still have a spirit. So have you. Only you're at war with yourself, Pat . . . and the first duty in the age of survival is to steer clear of self-destruction . . . and to accept yourself as you are.

Lloyd *reaches out to* **Pat**.

Pat   But that's not what I am . . .

Lloyd   I don't believe you.

Pat   I'm not.

Lloyd   Did you guess? . . .

Pat   Not till just now.

Lloyd   You didn't take evasive action.

Pat   I did. I separated the bed.

Lloyd   Not by much.

Pat   That would have seemed . . . unfriendly.

Lloyd *(amused)*   My God! That's very British of you! And you're not angry . . .

Pat   Why should I be?

Lloyd   Because I've been behaving like I'm interested in your soul and now all I want is your body.

There's a provocation here that **Pat** *doesn't rise to.*

Pat   I'm sorry. I'm just not . . .

Lloyd   A fag? A fruit?

Pat   No.

Lloyd   Sure?

Pat   I think I'm sure . . .

Lloyd   Think you're sure!

Pat   I wish I could say I was . . . but I can't . . .

Lloyd   You're up against the wire, ain't you? Staring at me like you stared at that Russian in the woods you told me about. Struck dumb by the 'enemy'. And now you've stumbled across another enemy, Pat . . . and the wire and the searchlights and the towers are just as real as they are in the Grunewald. Only our wire . . . the wire between you and me runs everywhere. On your side men want sex like wanting their mothers . . . they want softness and comfort. On this side it's flint and steel and it burns like fire . . . and you'd be transformed by it, my sweet friend. The thing about this wire is you can step through it. Come on . . . frontiers are for crossing.

Pat *takes his hand away.*

Pat   I can't. In the end there's something that stops me.

Lloyd   The guys in the machine-gun towers. Fine! *Finito!* Let's not wrestle with this any more. I tell you what we'll do, old chum . . . we'll get some sleep.

Pat   And yet . . . why is there a corner of me that could?

Lloyd   There was a corner of you that could have spoken to the Russian. No. You've had your moment. That's all you get. But we'll not fall out about it. I'll have the bed.

Pat (*hard*)   No! You have the mattress!

Lloyd   OK, OK. Good night, my friend. Sleep well.

Lloyd *wraps himself in the sheet and is absolutely still.* **Pat** *waits, then* **Pat** *turns off the light and eases himself on to the bedstead. He stares at* **Lloyd**.

Pat (*to audience*)   When Pat looks back to this moment . . . over half a century ago . . . squatting on that squirming bed . . . he sees himself, open-eyed in the dark, while Lloyd just seemed to roll over into sleep . . . and he remembers it now for what it was . . . just a plain act of cowardice.

Fade to black.

Scene Three

Mid-morning the next day, Sunday. **Pat** *and* **Lloyd** *are not present.*
Geoff, **Clive** *and* **Dilke**, *the military police sergeant, last seen on
Hanover station, are on stage. They have entered very quietly and now
stand like a tribunal, very still, taking a careful look around the room.
The mattress has been left on the floor. The bedstead still has the
blankets and cushions on it.*

Dilke *moves quietly to the garden doors and looks out.* **Geoff** *is
trying to contain his anger. He keeps his voice low.*

Geoff Has he heard us?

Dilke No, sir.

Clive We should search his things, sir.

Geoff Yes, of course. Carry on, Sergeant.

The sergeant goes to where **Pat**'s *battledress blouse is draped on a
chair back and searches the pockets. Checking through* **Pat**'s *paybook
he finds a slip of paper. He shows them to* **Geoff** *and* **Clive**, *then
opens* **Pat**'s *case, still searching. During this,* **Clive** *carefully inspects
the noticeboard. Finally, the sergeant shows them the copy of Turgenev's*
Fathers and Sons.

Dilke And this, sir . . .

Geoff I've seen that.

Dilke The flyleaf, sir.

Geoff *looks at the flyleaf and reads something there. He gives a
wearied reaction and passes it to* **Clive** *who reads it more
thoughtfully.*

Geoff Get him in.

Dilke *gives a fractional glance towards* **Clive** *and gets the smallest
of nods.*

Dilke (*calls*)   Sergeant Harford! Officer present! At the
double! Move yourself!

Pat, *dazed and nervous, enters from the garden. He's in shirtsleeve order, shirt unbuttoned, no beret.*

Dilke   You're improperly dressed, Sergeant! Button your shirt . . . Find your hat and put your boots and gaiters on!

Pat   What's happened, sir?

Geoff   Don't ask what's happened! Do it!

Pat *fishes around for his hat, boots and gaiters, and gets them on.* **Geoff** *is inwardly enraged by his every action.*

This morning . . . two in the morning . . . in Hanover I had a call from the Charlottenburg Military Police post here. They told me you had been seen leaving the charity ball at Reichskanzlerplatz, at twenty past midnight, with an American serviceman. He walked with you back to this centre, from all appearances to spend the night. D'you disagree with any of that?

Pat   No, sir . . . but . . .

Geoff   The military police asked me whether you had authorisation to bring British or non-British personnel to this centre. I said most definitely not. D'you agree?

Pat   I'm not sure we spoke about that, sir . . .

Pat *is desperate under the pressure of the three men.* **Geoff** *calms himself.*

Geoff   Why did you ask him here?

Clive   Sir!

Clive *is alarmed that* **Geoff** *may blunder into questioning that allows* **Pat** *off the hook.*

Geoff   Yes, Staff?

Clive *decides, since the question is asked, to let it ride.*

Clive   I'm sorry. Go ahead, sir.

Geoff (*sarcastically*)   Thank you. (*To* **Pat**.) Why did you ask him here?

Pat   He'd missed his last transport back to base.

Clive   Is that what you're telling us, or is it what he told you?

Pat   He told me, Staff . . .

Clive   To say that if you were asked?

Pat   I'm sorry? . . .

Clive   Did he suggest that that could be his excuse if anyone stopped you?

Pat   It's what happened. There was a US Army special bus service from the dance to American units. He missed the last one.

Dilke   May I, Staff? What time was the last one?

Pat   Midnight.

Dilke   How d'you know?

Pat   He told me.

Clive   He tell you anything else . . . ?

Clive *continues to stare at him encouragingly, as though he might offer something more.* **Pat**, *the shock of it all hitting him, doesn't respond.* **Geoff** *grows impatient, to* **Clive**'s *annoyance.* **Clive** *is trying to get* **Pat** *to talk unprompted.*

Geoff   What were you doing in the dance hall? You were on duty here!

Pat   I just wanted to look in, sir.

Geoff *flicks through the log.*

Geoff   You say here in the log: '19.30 hours, to HQ mess for evening meal. Returned 21.30 hours.' You didn't go there, did you? We checked.

Pat   Sir . . . you allowed me two hours for supper. I wasn't hungry and I thought it would be all right to use the time on something else.

Geoff   This is a false entry!

Pat   Yes, sir . . . technically . . .

Geoff   Don't 'technically' me!

Dilke   Do up that gaiter, Sergeant!

Pat *has to crouch to fasten a loose strap.* **Geoff** *makes introductions:*

Geoff   I think you've met Staff Sergeant Burns. Also Sergeant Dilke who drove me from Hanover . . . three hours through the night . . . He tells me he checked you on to the Berlin train at Hanover station five weeks ago. If only you'd never reached your destination, Sergeant! If only you'd been spirited away there and then!

Clive *indicates that he will take over.*

Clive (*to* **Pat**)   Did you dance?

Pat *can't focus on the question.*

Clive   When you got there, did you dance?

Pat   No . . .

Clive   Why not? You were very keen to go.

Pat   There weren't enough women, Staff. I couldn't find a partner.

Clive   So what did you do?

Pat   Had a drink . . .

Clive   On your own?

Pat   I met Corporal Jackson.

Clive   As you'd arranged to . . .

Pat   No! I'd never seen him before.

Clive What did you do?

Pat We just talked. (*Then:*) What's happened to him?

Dilke Did he write this?

*He shows the slip of paper he found in **Pat**'s jacket pocket.*

'Corporal Lloyd Jackson, 26th Infantry, McNair Barracks, Wilmersdorf'? Did he?

Pat Yes.

Clive He wrote it down for you?

Pat Yes.

Geoff He was lying!

Dilke There's no Corporal Lloyd Jackson known to the 26th. Nor to any of the US units in Berlin. He was also lying last night when he said he'd missed his last transport. The Americans had a bus leaving Reichskanzlerplatz on the hour, every hour, right through the night.

Pat What is he? A deserter?

Clive Nice try, Sergeant. When did you first meet him?

Pat Last night . . .

Clive The other time . . .

Pat Which other time?

Clive When you first got to Berlin. Or did you meet him before you came here? Did you meet him in Hanover?

*Clive is disorientating him. He appeals to **Geoff**.*

Pat Sir . . . I can't grasp all this . . .

Geoff That's because you're so pathetic, Sergeant. I doubt if you could grasp anything of any significance. The man wasn't American! He was German! What's more, East German. Have you grasped that, Sergeant? Your 'American' was a bloody agent for Soviet military intelligence!

Clive *winces at this ham-fisted approach.* **Dilke** *exchanges a look with him, as though getting* **Clive***'s permission to explain.*

Dilke   My military police colleagues at this end suspected this possibility last night. It's a known way of getting into British bases . . . passing yourself off as American. Helps to cover up ignorance of our regulations. Getting in as a guest is one of the few ways it can be done.

Clive   But you knew that, didn't you?

Pat   No.

Dilke   Same in the American sector. There they'd pose as British or French . . . So, you were put under observation last night . . . seen leaving with him this morning at about nine fifteen, walking with him to the S Bahn, where you left him and returned here. Yes?

Pat   He can't be German!

Clive   Why not?

Pat   Everything about him . . . his uniform . . .

Clive   You can buy a dozen US uniforms on the black market. It's a steady trade.

Dilke   After you left him he was followed on to the train . . . not the southbound S Bahn to Wilmersdorf, which he would have taken if genuine . . . but east towards Friedrichstrasse and the Soviet sector. No doubt he would have gone to a contact and changed clothes on the way. Unlucky for us he realised he was being tailed and tried to get off. So our men had to arrest him . . . which was a pity. If he hadn't seen them he might have led them to something interesting.

Geoff   You invited him into a British base . . . this is a British base. He is an agent in the pay of a hostile power.

Pat   But . . . what would he hope to find here?

Clive   You mean: what could he possibly learn at an Army Education Centre?

Geoff *is wary and unamused.* **Clive** *crosses to the noticeboard.*

Clive   Well, for example: here, openly displayed, is a list of every educational officer and NCO in the Berlin garrison, accompanied by the relevant unit and address . . . phone numbers too! Put it the other way round: a complete up-to-date list of almost every British Army unit in the garrison.

Geoff *is clearly embarrassed.*

Dilke   He could sell that. The Soviets always like to bring their info up to date.

Clive (*intending this for* **Geoff**)   And, no doubt, there are other documents around here that would be equally useful to him.

Pat   Where is he now?

Clive   Here.

Pat   Here!

Dilke   Next door. We'll need you to identify him. We still don't know his real name so you will identify him as the man who called himself Corporal Lloyd Jackson. Understood, Sergeant?

Pat   I have to see him?

They treat this with contempt.

Geoff   Maybe I should hand you back to Major Rogers after all. He chose you for this duty, not me. You should be on his carpet not mine.

Clive *adopts a 'confidential' tone to* **Geoff**.

Clive   No, no, sir. You asked me specially to come in on this so we could 'keep it on the island', not spread it about . . . and that suits me too. That man could turn out useful to us if we play it right. (*To* **Pat**.) As for you, Sergeant, this is the stage where, if there's anything you've concealed, tell us now and it'll all go in your favour. Anything you want to say?

Pat   I can't believe he wasn't who he said he was . . .

Clive *gives him up.*

Clive   All right, Sergeant Dilke . . . .what have we got?

Dilke   What we don't have is actual evidence of espionage. Anything he took from here he may have shoved out of the train window when he sensed he'd got company. (*To* **Pat**.) Did you see him with a camera at any time?

Pat   No . . .

Clive   Did you see him writing any notes?

Pat   Well, he had a diary.

Clive   What did it look like? What colour?

Pat   Black . . .

Clive   How big?

Pat   Size of a diary . . .

He makes the shape of a small notebook. **Dilke** *goes to phone and dials a number.*

Geoff   How d'you know it was a diary?

Pat   He said so, sir.

Geoff (*wearily*)   Oh my God!

Dilke (*on phone*)   Sergeant Dilke here. I have a description of a notebook he was carrying. It's a small black book . . . size and appearance of a diary . . . right? Yes. I'm at the centre.

Puts phone down. **Clive** *crosses to noticeboard and ponders it.*

Clive (*to* **Pat**)   Did you see him taking an interest in this noticeboard?

Pat   We had a joke about it, yes. The names of our regiments. The Eleventh Hussars . . .

Geoff   What about the Eleventh Hussars?

Pat   The name. It struck him as funny.

Clive   Did he write anything down?

Pat   He put that down, yes. Just a joke!

Clive   Did you sleep last night?

Pat   I took a while to get off . . .

Clive   Did you sleep?

Pat   Yes.

Clive   On the mattress or the bed?

Pat   Why? . . .

Clive   Mattress or bed?

Pat (*intimidated*)   Bed.

Clive   The bed creaks. If he was on the mattress he had more opportunity.

Pat   What d'you mean?

Clive   To get up while you were asleep. He'd make less sound! He could take that list out into another room, put the light on and copy it . . . Afterwards he could pin it up again when he crept back in.

Dilke   Anything you reckon might be missing, sir?

Geoff   I'm not sure. I've sent a car round for Ilse. She'll check.

Clive   I'm going to bring him in. (*To* **Pat**.) You witness what he said and did last night. We've got to make him believe that we have the evidence to charge him now . . . just with what we've got. Then he'll do a deal.

Pat   What d'you mean, 'witness'?

Clive   It means, Sergeant, that he made notes from that board in his little black book. You saw him do it.

Pat   No!

Geoff   What d'you mean, 'no'?

Pat   It wasn't like that!

Geoff   Jesus to God! A man who sells information that could cost the lives of soldiers in this garrison and you say 'It wasn't like that'!

Clive *signals to* **Dilke** *that he wants the cellophane wallet of evidence. He takes out the book.*

Clive (*To* **Pat**)   In the flyleaf of your novel by Turgenev, this is written: 'Dear son, Remember the way forward.' Is it your father's writing?

Pat   Yes.

Clive   He then puts a quotation: 'Every cook has to learn how to govern the state.' And after it, the initials: V.I.L. Who would that be?

Pat (*mumbles*)   Lenin . . .

Clive   Who?

Pat   Lenin.

Clive   Vladimir Ilich Lenin?

Pat   Yes.

Clive   Is your father a communist?

Pat   You can quote Lenin without being a communist.

Clive   Is he a communist?

Pat   No . . .

Clive *detects a wobble.*

Clive   I can find out. All it needs is a phone call.

Pat   He quit in 1940 . . . when Stalin had the pact with Hitler.

Clive   Ah yes. Not many cooks running the state under Stalin were there? What about you? Are you in the party?

Pat   I'm not in any party!

Clive   Well, you're in this fucking party! This is a party dedicated to doing what has to be done . . . and we don't waste time in voting. (*To* **Dilke**.) Bring him in . . . (*Then he remembers protocol.*) Oh, with your permission, sir . . .

Geoff   Of course . . .

Dilke *exits.*

Clive (*to* **Pat**)   Don't speak unless I ask you to. Confine yourself to answering the question . . . and co-operate, Sergeant, or you're up shit creek.

Dilke *enters, leading* '**Lloyd Jackson**' *who is handcuffed and without his tunic. His shirt is dirt-stained, his face heavily bruised down one side. He doesn't look at* **Pat**.

Clive (*to* **Dilke**)   Anything?

Dilke   Nothing.

Clive   Has Staff Cullen arrived?

Dilke   Yes, he's had a look at him. He's on the phone now.

Clive (*to* **Pat**)   Do you recognise this man, Sergeant Harford?

Pat *stares at* **Lloyd** *with growing anger.* **Clive** *waits, then:*

Clive   Is this the man you encountered at Reichskanzlerplatz and brought here last night? The man who gave his name as Corporal Lloyd Jackson, US Army? Is this the man?

Pat   He doesn't look the same.

Clive   Don't fuck about! Excuse me, sir . . .

Geoff   Answer the question, Sergeant!

Pat   He doesn't look the same . . .

Clive   Don't be stupid!

Pat   He's got a bruised face!

Geoff, *troubled, looks enquiringly at* **Dilke**.

Geoff   Sergeant?

Pat   The man I met didn't have a bruised face.

Dilke   He resisted arrest, sir.

Enter **Fraser**, *dressed in smart civilian casual clothes as before. He holds a piece of paper.*

Fraser   Sir . . .

Geoff   Not now, Staff!

Clive   Staff Cullen's been making enquiries for us, sir. Got the name?

Fraser   He's Emil Voss. (*Spells.*) V-O-S-S . . . Soviet sector . . . lives near Friedrichstrasse. He was brought up in the States . . . in Baltimore. His father worked there in shipping before the war.

He hands the paper to **Clive** *who glances at it and passes it to* **Geoff**.

Clive   That your name? Emil Voss?

Pat   Lloyd!

Clive   Shut up! (*To the prisoner.*) I'm going to ask you again. If you remain silent that will be taken as a denial and then I can't help you. There will be no possibility of any other arrangement. Is your name Emil Voss?

Lloyd/Emil   OK.

Clive   Oh, we make contact! Emil . . . d'you recognise
Sergeant Harford?

Emil   *Ja.* Natürlich.

Fraser   Staff . . .

Fraser *wants to add to the information he has given but* **Clive** *cuts
him short.*

Clive   One moment. Sergeant Harford will testify that you
posed as an American serviceman in order to gain access to
a British Army establishment with the intention of
information gathering and passing the results to a foreign
power . . .

Emil *cuts across, indicating* **Pat**.

Emil   *Er weiss warum ich gekommen bin.*

Clive   *Bitte?*

Geoff   What?

Clive   D'you follow that, Sergeant? He says you know
why he came.

Pat (*softly*)   I asked you to come . . . I invited you!

Pat *tries to make eye contact with him but* **Emil** *stares straight
ahead.*

Emil   OK. I'll tell you. I'm homosexual. I went to the
dance at Reichskanzlerplatz to find a partner. I wore the
uniform for that purpose and for that purpose alone. I sat in
a side bar where homosexuals make contact. I met the
sergeant and he invited me back to this house. There was no
question of information gathering . . . I know nothing of
information gathering. It was purely a sexual matter. OK?

Fraser   Oh dear, oh dear! I was afraid he might put up
one of those.

Geoff   Take him next door!

Clive   But, sir! It's a blind, that's all it is . . . a blind!

Clive *leaps at* **Emil** *and presses his fingers into his neck.* **Pat** *tries to pull him off.*

Emil   Shit!

Pat   Leave him!

Dilke   Stand still!

Pat (*to* **Clive**)   Do it to me! Do it to me!

Geoff   Stop this!

Dilke (*to* **Clive**)   Watch it Staff! . . . (*To* **Pat**.) Three paces back!

Fraser   Now, gentlemen! King's Regulations. Let us get ourselves back to order! (*Then a quiet warning.*) Clive . . . (*Then.*) Sergeant Dilke . . .

Dilke   Yes, Staff . . .

Fraser   With your permission, sir, I suggest Sergeant Dilke takes this man quietly into the next room.

Geoff   No! An accusation has been made.

Fraser   It's not what it seems, sir . . .

Geoff   The prisoner said that Sergeant Harford invited him back for homosexual purposes . . .

Fraser   No, sir . . .

Clive   It's a ploy! A smokescreen!

Fraser   Been used before, sir . . .

Clive   Sodding bastard's trying to throw us off course!

Geoff (*resisting*)   I'm ordering Sergeant Harford to answer the accusation.

Pat *has made up his mind to oppose them. He fights to contain his rage and his fear.*

Pat   It's true, sir. That is why I invited him.

Geoff (*to* **Clive** *and* **Fraser**)   You hear this?

Fraser   Pat!

Geoff   Spell it out! Are you a queer?

Pat   I invited him back for what he said.

Fraser   It's not true, sir.

Geoff   Did you commit acts of gross indecency with that man?

Pat   Yes.

Clive (*to* **Pat**)   You play this game and I'll break you!

Geoff   Well, it's clear what has to happen now . . . .

Clive   Sir, please!

Geoff   He's just told me he's a homosexual . . . in which case it's an Ed Corps matter now and the first thing I have to do is inform Major Rogers on whose orders he was sent here for this duty.

Clive   But if you do that, sir, that monkey there has run circles round us. I honestly don't believe Sergeant Harford, sir.

Geoff   Don't be ridiculous. Who'd lie about being a pervert?

Clive   Sergeant Harford is lying, sir, and I think I know why. He comes to Berlin, newborn and pink as a squeaking piglet, just in time to miss the Soviet blockade that brought the people here, for the second time, to the edge of starvation and disease. But he, well fed and watered in the privileged comfort of a sergeant's mess . . . he thinks: surely we're exaggerating this cold war thing. To him, Emil . . . 'Lloyd' . . . is not the mortal enemy of his country but a fellow human who walks, talks and breathes just like we do. He's lying to protect him.

Geoff   What d'you say to that, Sergeant?

Pat   I say what I've said, sir.

Emil, *genuinely concerned that* **Pat** *should put himself in danger, becomes* **Lloyd** *again for a moment.*

Emil   But Pat! There's no need!

Dilke   Quiet! Don't speak unless questioned!

Clive (*to* **Pat**)   What's he mean, 'There's no need'?

Geoff   I've had enough of this! Sergeant Dilke, take the prisoner away.

Dilke   Yes, sir. (*To* **Emil**.) On your feet! (*Then, because* **Emil** *looks as though he might have more to say.*) No speaking! Out!

Emil   Survive, Pat! Survive!

Dilke *exits with* **Emil** *to the hall.*

Clive   I think even the prisoner's telling us it wasn't so, sir.

Geoff (*indicating* **Pat**)   He's admitted to an act of gross indecency! (*To* **Pat**.) Isn't that the case, Sergeant?

Pat   Yes, sir.

Geoff   You see! Good God! D'you expect me to ignore it? Order some transport. I want him out of here and to Major Roberts.

Clive   Sir . . . that man in there could be like gold dust to us, providing we can turn him and get him back to the East before his absence makes them suspicious. An inquiry into whether indecency took place would delay that, sir. It could put in danger a potential asset to British Military Intelligence in this garrison and I think a very poor view would be taken of that. I do really.

Geoff *is intimidated by the implication but doesn't know how to back down.*

Fraser   Sir . . . Why don't I have a word with Sergeant Harford . . . in private?

Clive   Now there's a good idea, sir.

Geoff (*to* **Fraser**)   D'you think he's . . . shamming?

Fraser   I'm sceptical, sir . . . but that's my way . . .

Geoff *is still reluctant.* **Clive** *deliberately lures him away.*

Clive   I reckon there's more we can extract from Emil and I'd appreciate your help next door, sir.

Geoff *is inwardly flattered to be invited to share an interrogation.*

Geoff (*to* **Pat**)   Well, you've got a chance to sort yourself out, Sergeant . . . and believe you me, it's the only chance you'll get. Take it.

Geoff *and* **Clive** *exit.* **Fraser** *drops the controlled manner.*

Fraser   What the hell went wrong last night?

Pat   Have you spoken to her?

Fraser   No! What happened?

Pat (*bitter*)   I thought you'd know.

Fraser   Pat . . . this is me. Not them. Me!

Pat   She never showed up.

Fraser   She must have done!

Pat   I was there!

Fraser   She'd be late . . . She's always late!

Pat   I waited forty-five minutes.

Fraser   And she never?

Pat *shakes his head.*

Fraser   Oh, stupid cow!

Pat   She obviously didn't want to . . .

Fraser   What did you do?

Pat   Hung around . . .

Fraser   Do you know why they leave me here to talk to you? It's to test you for genuine . . . because as far as they're concerned, I'm the expert . . .

Pat *begins to realise.*

Pat   Expert at what?

Fraser   Schoolie! I know you're not one. I knew it in the first five minutes of meeting you. (*Indicates* **Emil**.) He isn't one either.

Pat   Yes he is!

Fraser   It's an act. It's his way in. He's an impersonator. If you want to know what the genuine article is like it's sitting here in front of you.

Pat *is astonished, then suspects a trick.*

Pat   You're saying it . . .

Fraser   Yes, I'm saying it.

Pat   But you don't seem . . .

Fraser   Like one?

Pat   Yes.

Fraser   Thank you. I work quite hard at that. All the best fairies appear in disguise . . .

Pat   You said you had a girlfriend . . . You showed me a photo!

Fraser   Yes, good, isn't it?

Pat   Gisela . . .

Fraser   What's in a name? You should know that. Now listen, Pat . . . I may not have a 'she' but you do. I only have to tell them what took place here the night before last.

Pat   It didn't happen . . .

Fraser   She practically drew me a picture!

Pat It didn't happen!

Fraser Come on now, Pat. All they want is an answer
you can easily give. You never invited that man to share
your bed, did you?

Pat I've said what I've said.

Fraser You're wondering why I'm tolerated while you
have all this thrown at you? Well, you've got to know the
army. They'll tolerate poofters when it suits them. Especially
in the war. You could be more open about it then, with the
bullets flying. (*Then:*) What you have said, Pat, is 'yes' to
committing an act of gross indecency! You don't really
know what an act of gross indecency is, do you?

He tries to ease the tension.

Awe-inspiring phrase: 'Act of Gross Indecency'. Makes you
think of the old song: 'He rode up to the manor. He rode up
to the hall. Cor blimey! said the butler . . . He's come to
fuck us all!'

Pat responds slightly. **Fraser** *indicates next door.*

Fraser There are some things in this city you're not
going to learn unless you're 'one of us'. I serve my country,
Pat. I'm one of His Majesty's queers. The Royal Corps of
Poofters. *Pro Patria Posteriori.* I carry some clout . . . So I can
help you if you'll see sense.

Pat I've said it now.

Fraser Unsay it. Tell 'em the truth.

Pat Truth! What's truth to them? Who's on our side and
who isn't? Who's Red? Who's not? Who's East? Who's
West?

Fraser I think you liked him.

Pat looks at **Fraser** *helplessly.*

Pat Yes . . .

Fraser   Course you did. How else is he going to talk his way in?

Pat   I wanted him! I honestly did want him, Fraser . . . I did!

Fraser   Pat, you're going to make me jealous. Listen, I've seen men as straight as a three-foot rule, yet when the heat was on, when it was there in front of them, they just wanted to snatch the chance to bend . . . just that once in their lives; just once. But the fact remains, Pat, you didn't invite him back with you for sex. Did you?

Pat *won't answer.*

Fraser   Don't go down this path. You don't realise what they can do. I'm not just talking about prison, or discharge with dishonour. It's after that. They'll drop the word wherever you go. If you get a job they'll give them the whisper. If you marry they'll send your wife an unsigned tip-off. They want your head in a gas oven, or your body in a park lake.

But **Pat** *remains silent.*

Say it was his mistake. You accidentally went into that bar which is a well-known pick-up place. He thought it was on offer, when it wasn't.

Pat   No.

Fraser   Come on, Pat! You can see what Clive wants. The old routine. He's got one of theirs and he wants to get him facing both ways.

Pat   Well, he's not going to have my help.

Fraser   You know Geoff's sent for Ilse, don't you? She's on her way here now to check for things missing. And the moment she gets here and hears this she'll give you away. She won't be able to help herself! She'll tell them all because she'll think she's rescuing you. And then you'll be in a different kind of trouble, won't you, when Geoff learns she's been in your bed . . .

Pat   She hasn't!

Fraser   I think this city's affected you more than you know, Schoolie. You just want the chance to shout out about it, don't you? Save someone, no matter who. You've made your point and I admire you for it. I do. But I won't if you don't drop it now. It's enough, Schoolie. It's enough.

Enter **Geoff**, *followed by* **Clive**.

Geoff   We can't allow any more time for this. Are you ready to deny what he said?

Pat   No.

Clive   What d'you say, Fraser? Is he?

Fraser   Of course he isn't.

Clive (*to* **Pat**)   So deny it!

Pat   No.

Geoff   You realise that would be perjury in a court martial?

Clive   And we can soon make it one.

Pat *remains silent.* **Clive** *now pursues a deliberately harsh course.*

Clive   When you committed the act of gross indecency . . . You did commit an act of gross indecency, did you?

Fraser   No he didn't!

Pat   Yes.

Clive   Were you both naked?

Pat (*cautiously*)   Don't remember . . .

Clive (*indicating next door*)   He says you were.

Pat   All right . . . yes.

Clive   So you'd have seen his penis? Yes?

Pat   Yes.

Clive   Is his foreskin intact, or is it as the chosen people?

Pat   I don't remember.

Clive   All right. Undo your flies.

Geoff   Staff!

Clive   Sir . . . I have a description of his member from the prisoner and I need to see if it tallies!

Pat   I'm not circumcised, if that's what you want.

Clive   Sergeant, you say you're homosexual when you are not . . . so why should I believe anything that spews out of your slimy mouth? Show it.

Pat *unbuttons his flies.* **Geoff** *has moved away, embarrassed.*

Clive   Would you like to inspect it, sir?

Geoff   I've done so.

He motions **Pat** *to button up.*

Clive   Let's move on to the buggery. Who buggered who first?

Pat *won't answer.*

Clive   I'm talking about the one who did the initial inserting. Was it you or him?

No reply.

When you were the receiving party what position were you in? Show us your position! Was it all fours? Was it foetus? Were you upside down, over the bedstead . . . or in some more exotic configuration?

Geoff   Staff Burns . . . I want this done in the proper manner and in the proper place!

Clive *backs off.*

Fraser If I may say so, I think Staff Burns is doing you a favour, Sergeant, in showing you the way things will go if you stay on this course. You'll have tribunals worse than this. It's the detail they love.

Enter **Dilke**.

Dilke Excuse me, sir. Fräulein Bucher is here. Shall she wait?

Pat *is unnerved by the news.*

Geoff She needs to check whether anything was stolen.

Clive Then let her do that, sir.

Fraser *tries to give* **Pat** *time to recant.*

Fraser Could we have a moment, sir?

Geoff What for, Staff?

Fraser *has to give up on* **Pat**.

Fraser Just to be sure we've all collected ourselves . . .

Geoff *gives him a heavy look, then nods to* **Dilke** *who shows in* **Ilse**. *She is dressed for travel in old mountain or ski wear with rucksack on her back and a suitcase in her hand. She glances at* **Pat** *in a tense manner.*

Geoff Good morning, Fräulein Bucher. Has Sergeant Dilke explained?

Ilse He said there could be papers missing.

Dilke I've briefed the Fräulein, sir. I've told her the man broke in last night while Sergeant Harford was sleeping, sir.

Geoff And . . . ?

Dilke And what, sir?

Geoff *realizes no more should be said.*

Geoff Yes. All right . . .

Dilke *exits.* **Geoff** *speaks to* **Ilse**.

Geoff   Start with the noticeboard. (*Then:*) Why the suitcase?

Ilse   I was just going somewhere.

She begins to check the noticeboard.

Geoff   Where?

Ilse   Somewhere. (*Continues to check the board.*) Everything OK here.

She checks the desks, all the time trying not to catch the eye of **Pat** *or* **Fraser**. *She picks up a wad of papers.*

I don't know how many I had of these, so I don't know if any are gone.

Clive   What are they?

Ilse   Spelling tests.

Geoff   Yes . . . well . . .

Clive   Inside the desk.

Ilse   It was locked. I locked it.

Clive   He could have unlocked it and locked it again.

She searches her desk. **Geoff** *does the same with his.*

Ilse   No. Everything is here. The old problem. They either get it on film or make notes. (*To* **Geoff**.) You haven't opened your mail.

Geoff   What mail?

Ilse *indicates the buff envelope on his desk.*

Pat   Yes . . . it came yesterday.

Geoff   Speak up!

Pat   It came yesterday, sir. I put it there for you.

Geoff   You should have said.

Pat   I was going to, sir.

Geoff, *annoyed, opens it.*

Geoff (*reads and sighs*)   It's from burials . . . about those two in the garden. There's been a mistake. It turns out to be the garden four houses down.

Fraser   What a shame. I'd got quite fond of them . . . We should have given them names.

Geoff   They're not there!

Fraser   No, sir . . .

Clive   They frequently aren't.

Ilse   Well that's Berlin for you. Even the dead are displaced persons. (*Then.*) D'you want me any more?

Clive   No.

Geoff   Yes!

Dilke *enters from the hall, pleased with himself. He singles out* **Clive**.

Dilke   Staff . . .

Clive   What you got?

Dilke   Come and see.

Clive *exits with* **Dilke**. **Geoff** *is torn, feeling they are leaving him out, yet wanting to talk to* **Ilse**. *He decides he must find out what's happening next door.*

Geoff (*to* **Ilse**)   I'll want a word with you!

He exits to hall. **Ilse** *is released from the strain of not being able to speak to* **Pat** *and* **Fraser**.

Ilse   Oh Pat!

Fraser   *Liebchen!* What happened?

Ilse   I was afraid! (*To* **Pat**.) I couldn't bring myself to come to the dance. I was afraid that we'd be seen! I rang you but by then you'd gone!

Pat Don't worry about it.

Ilse But I do! I wanted to be with you so much!

She kisses and embraces **Pat**. **Fraser** *indicates the door and the possibility that the others will return.*

Fraser (*to* **Pat**)   Well . . . I told you.

Ilse If I'd come this wouldn't have happened! What did he do to you? Did he hurt you?

Pat No. No he didn't. I'm OK. Don't worry.

Ilse Oh Fraser, this sergeant! He comes here . . . And he tells me how he has lived an ordinary life at home in England. And I'm thinking: where is my ordinary life . . . my father . . . my mother? Where can I find it now? So I'm going. I sat up all night and decided. I'm going . . .

Fraser Where?

Ilse Home. To Grossau. To my village.

Fraser To the East? You can't do that!

Ilse I'm going to find my mother if she's still alive. You see, I thought the best way was to earn money here and pay people to look for her. And I did. I paid people who do this. But they have not found her and I keep telling myself: oh well, I must earn more money and pay more people and more people! But all I'm doing is running away all over again . . . It's me! I must go back. I must find her.

Fraser You can't do it!

Ilse I must! She could be sick, or starving . . . or lost her mind. Some people say women were taken to Stettin to work in the hospital. She could be there! I have never dared go back to look for her. The big fear . . . my real fear . . . is that I will have that on my conscience all my life.

Fraser Listen . . . I'll get people to look for her . . .

Ilse   And I sit here and do nothing? Even the man last night, coming in here to find things he can sell. He does something!

Pat   What d'you mean?

Ilse   He helps his family!

Fraser   They've all got someone, somewhere who's trying to keep body and soul together.

Pat   And that's why he was doing it?

Ilse   Of course! What d'you expect people to do? And if he can come West to do it, I can go East!

Pat   But you can't cross the Russian zone!

Ilse   Yes I can.

Fraser   But your home's not there any more! All that territory's been given to Poland! They're throwing Germans out.

Ilse   Well, I shall squeeze in. I have Polish friends in Grossau.

Fraser   They won't be so friendly now. You'll need papers.

Ilse   I got papers. They're OK . . . I paid good money. And cigarettes, I got plenty of cigarettes for bribes . . . Chesterfields!

Fraser   How d'you think you'll get there?

Ilse   A girlfriend of mine in Weissensee in East Berlin . . . her uncle drives a truck. He'll take me as far as Stettin. He goes today. And, listen . . . he won't take anything for it. He says we should all help one another. That is actually what he says!

Fraser *is at a loss.*

Pat   You were going to America.

Ilse (*satirically*)   Oh America! America!

Fraser   You'll be stopped by the Russians before you've gone a mile.

Ilse   So I shall speak Russian. I'll have them making tea for me!

Fraser   But if you go over there you'll have nothing! They've got nothing!

Ilse   I can do a lot with nothing. I was here in '45! (*She breaks into passionate German.*) Ich war damals hier! Ich bin immer noch hier! Glaubst du ich kann das nicht verkraften? (*'I was here then! I'm still here! D'you think I can't manage it?'*) Anyway, I miss my little village. You should see it, Pat. It's such a beautiful place.

Fraser   In case you haven't noticed it's communist now.

Ilse   It's just a little village. It's just grass and trees! Is a communist tree different from a capitalist tree?

She hands a letter to **Fraser**.

Give this to Geoff. It tells him all that needs to be done. I must go before he comes back . . .

Fraser   You'll be owed some wages . . .

Ilse   Buy wine with it. Have a party! I tell you, Fraser, I'll do one American thing . . . I'll teach them to jitterbug.

Fraser   In Siberia.

Ilse   Yes . . . in Siberia!

She kisses **Fraser**, *then approaches* **Pat**.

Pat   You don't speak . . .

Pat   *Ya sdayoos* . . .

She looks as though she might weaken for a moment, then picks up her case and rucksack.

Ilse   *Ya sdayoos.*

She exits through the garden.

Fraser   Stupid bint! Why didn't she phone me first? At least I could have arranged it properly.

He makes a helpless gesture.

You know, I sometimes have these little dreams that I'm as hetero as you are, Schoolie. I have this fantasy about being the father of a daughter . . . and she's lovely to me. She doesn't give me pain or grief or make trouble from arsehole to breakfast time! Oh, the silly cow!

Hears the others in the next room.

Don't tell them where I've gone. I'll drive her. At least I can get her through CheckPoint Charlie!

He exits through the garden.

*Enter **Geoff** with **Clive** following.*

Geoff   Good God! Is no one guarding you?

Pat   No, sir. Sorry about that, sir.

Geoff   Where's Ilse?

Pat   She's gone, sir.

Geoff   Where?

Pat *thinks a moment.*

Pat   Home.

Geoff *thinks he means to her apartment and jumps to the conclusion that **Fraser** has engineered it.*

Geoff   Staff Cullen! He heard me say I wanted her to stay!

Sound of a Volks starting up.

Cullen!

He exits through the house to stop them.

Clive *weighs up **Pat** very carefully.*

Clive   This thinking war, that you say doesn't . . . or shouldn't . . . exist has moved on a notch. We've found Emil's little book . . . the one you called a diary, which in a sense it is.

He shows the little black book, now in a cellophane packet.

Lying on the grass verge this side of Tiergarten station. What's in it is all the evidence we need . . . including, wouldn't you know, the list of Berlin garrison army units from the board over there.

Pat   Is he going to work for you?

Clive *ignores this.*

Clive   He's put some other interesting things in the book . . . a note about yourself. He says you showed sympathy with the socialist cause and that, at one point, you withdrew your oath of loyalty to the King. Has he got that right?

Pat *has to struggle with his fear of what they might do with this.*

Pat   Just something I did in my mind . . .

Clive   Haven't I told you: it's the things of the mind we're fighting about? Look at his last note!

He holds the book in front of him and indicates a sentence in it.

I'll translate: 'This man is extremely disaffected and might prove a useful contact.'

Pat   I'm not a communist!

Clive   No! You haven't the guts. D'you know what Captain Wirral would do if he could read what's in here? (*Indicates book.*) He'd want you tried for treason. But if he did that, Emil Voss would have to take the stand. Now that wouldn't suit me at all. Voss may be low level but he has a direct line to Soviet intelligence. We need him back over there with some nice things to tell them and we want it now! So I don't want your balls-aching, half-baked gestures getting in the way. You are going to sign an Official Secrets Act, undertaking, Sergeant . . . not to divulge any knowledge of him whatsoever . . . meeting him . . . bringing him here . . . all of it. In return we'll keep this book among friends.

Pat What'll happen, Staff?

Clive You stay silent and, if I have my way, all you'll have against you is absent on duty and falsifying the log. But always remember . . . I'll still have this . . .

He waves the black book.

Pat Will I be discharged?

Clive No. You'll serve out your time so we know where you are and what you're doing. Captain Wirral will insist to Major Roberts that you're demoted and returned to the UK. In his opinion you're not fit to teach anyone, let alone soldiers. Right . . . you are now formally under arrest. Take the laces out of your boots and give me your belt, beret and gaiters.

Pat *kneels to undo the gaiters.*

Problem with people like you is that you believe peace is the natural condition of the human race. It's not and never has been. Peace is only the gaps between wars . . . and wars are where humanity achieves its full potential. Well, you'll have time to contemplate that where you're going. It'll be very peaceful.

Clive *stares ahead of him suddenly 'outside time'.*

The actor playing **Pat** *is gradually isolated. He speaks to the audience.*

Pat He said . . . what Staff Sergeant Burns did probably saved his sanity. He was posted back home as an army clerk to a remote vehicle depot in the middle of Norfolk. Gradually, under those wide skies, he pulled back from the brink . . . his anger and confusion, his secret . . . and his alone.

Clive, *now in real time, exists with:*

Clive   Sergeant Dilke! Take over the prisoner!

Pat   After the army, Pat *did* qualify as an architect. He married and had a cherished family. Lived and worked, not brilliantly but well enough, through all those years from then to now . . . through Staff Sergeant Burns' wars and threats of wars . . . through the time the wall came down and the Love Parade began and the red dust blew away as though it had never been . . . and on through more wars, massacres, cleansings and genocides. The roll call of ruined cities never stopped.

A suggestion of movement as he 'travels' to Berlin.

Then, come the Millennium, now retired, Pat did what he'd feared to do for so long . . . he returned to Berlin. There was an architectural conference to serve as an excuse. In Charlottenburg, the house he hadn't seen for fifty years was glistening with fresh paint, now the offices of a marketing consultancy . . . the rose garden a directors' car park. At the S Bahn station, where he'd said goodbye to Lloyd, he took a train to Potzdammerplatz to see the new Berlin being built.

A feeling of him standing on a bright, high observation platform.

From an observation platform you could view the biggest construction site in Europe . . . a vast Rift Valley of excavations, constantly fed by lines of zebra striped concrete trucks. There were finished buildings too . . . fragile towers of tinted glass, staring across that vanished frontier where, once, two vast empires of the mind were kept in place by soldiers.

He looked east . . . what his generation had called '*the* east' . . . The cellar where Ilse had hidden could only be a few streets away. His spirit went out to her. Wherever she was, he saw her, far away from this shining city, crouching in the dirt, butchering a dog to stay alive.

He turns from 'the east'.

Then it struck him that, all those years ago, he'd never asked her what the dog tasted like. So he'd ask her now! Why not? Out of the dead rubble of unanswered questions, it sprang up like a flower! 'What did the dog taste like?' He chanted it over and over in his head, crowding out all other thoughts, beating time to it in his heart: What did the dog . . . what did the dog . . . what did the dog taste like?